STRAY DOGS

&

IRREVERSIBLE CARS

BOOKS BY JAMES GRABILL

Stray Dogs and Irreversible Cars (poetry), Atmosphere Press, 2024

Schoenberg in the Troposphere (poetry), Cyberwit, 2023

Eye of the Spiral (poems), UnCollected Press, 2022

Reverberation of the Genome (poems), Cyberwit, 2021

Branches Shaken by Light (poems), Cyberwit, 2020

Sea-Level Nerve, Book Two (prose poems), Wordcraft of Oregon, 2015

Sea-Level Nerve, Book One (prose poems), Wordcraft of Oregon, 2014

October Wind (poems), Sage Hill Press, 2006

Finding the Top of the Sky (creative nonfiction, poems), Lost Horse Press, 2005

An Indigo Scent after Rain (poems), Lynx House Press, 2003

Lame Duck Eternity (wild poems), 26 Books chapbook, 2000

Listening to the Leaves Form (poems, prose poems), Lynx House Press, 1997

Through the Green Fire (creative nonfiction, poems), Holy Cow! Press, 1995

Poem Rising Out of the Earth and Standing Up in Someone (poems), Lynx House
Press, 1994 (Oregon Book Award, 1995)

In the Coiled Light (poems), NRG chapbook, 1985

To Other Beings (poems), Lynx House Press, 1981

Clouds Blowing Away (poems), Seizure and kayak Press, 1976

One River (a reverie of poems), Momentum Press, 1975

STRAY DOGS
&
IRREVERSIBLE CARS

JAMES GRABILL

POEMS

atmosphere press

CONTENTS

In nature's economy the currency is not money, it is life.
– Vandana Shiva

I.

Extinction is the rule.
Survival is the exception.
— **Carl Sagan**

When you are already in Detroit,
you don't have to take a bus to get there.
— **Ram Dass**

WAVE OF LIGHT

As night tills ancestral symbiosis inherited
a mile down in dutiful strength, the weathered
species, as complex as the Parthenon blazing
then indwelling, quick in a surgeon's fingers,

has been touched by the sunlit glaciers draining
and those train blasts through the summer night
or the 3 p.m. gravity of conditions on the ground
sunlight is reaching, as boxcars of bleached coral

crumbled now to bone dust are passing, clattering,
and security cars hauling payloads of single zero
past cedars in their flame, opening through air
in which a bear whimpers as the north ice melts

lightning inches in each pulse of a violet eyelash,
the instantaneous continuum remarkable as bees
still chance the completion of an individual cycle,
embarking on their travels in the sky unfolding

into blossoms, the infrared halves of the sun
reaching shapes on the planet, ruining the stone
palaces with mammoth consequences as fingers
intertwine, and rock glistens from underground

in intricate flicker woodpecker living feathers,
for the eyeball iris makes its purple-blue burst
from seed into what stays unthinkable beauty,
what kneels its grief onto hillsides, as a woman

works a small spot-lit stage, dancing the place
filled by neon pulsing synthesis, as gravity lets her
move in a split-second nautilus of this planetary
unfolding, sunlight roaring to where the grackle

stretches her wings when she's back, whistling
to another, bobbing her head, talking grackle
maybe to say what she's seen, overflowing light
she's become, reverberating in splashes of corn

the moment that's ending its labor in solidness,
with evening blanketed by action, as sunlight
continues to go into what might have felt empty
in time, and will in time be filled again, rounded

back to a sphere with human overpopulation still
sweeping in past umbilical doors to the next stage
the mind has for its coast, entering the exquisite
eye within each cell of the eye, for the light this is.

SHADOW OF THE FIRES

I.

Great barrier reefs of simple TV
let anxious fish through to last church suppers
(with the sounds of scraping forks on china).
Voices in the center of the country
thicken into reaching vegetable plants
in a garden over tombs of the dead,
with sudden side views of great grandmothers,
the tinkling of glasses of icewater,
the small white gloves floating down to the floor,
the no-miles swaying half the crosses round
with hour hands, and half the men now gone.

We lose ourselves in basements of this grave.
Gravity grows inside someone gone west.
Kandinsky spirals centers of action
punctured by steeples, through which three moons drift.
Chagall upturns the barn into some boat
a cow will pull because it loves to live,
with slow rollings from pre-German drummers as
the nearby twelfth century hovers.

II.

Blue-black sisters run from bonfire shadows.
Melting French children from the '40s watch.
Great cathedral organ masters thunder.
Crossbow artists wait for that perfect twitch.
Half-aimed houses blanket fields in graveyards,
blast sounds of furnaces, engines, horses,
wooden wheels revolving on this axis

of the no-storm, long wagons shimmying
as soothsayers might bespeak unison
through no-miles, ground-granted, chanted maskings
looming in starlight still reaching the Earth.

A puritan ancestral grandmother
pushes her bonneted head into view
an inch away, her scorn for the clock's sin
just being there, just here in this one hour.
We might as well make noises of the beasts
for all we know of God's great purity.
The leper angels clean up after death.
The body of sick skin is pushed back down
toward opened throats that will swallow the world.

                    III.
Pollock swirls his paints above the darkness
and waves electric light where none began.
Birds' nests form; flights of birds are seen through time.
Whitened knots are tied as shadows loosen.
A badger yawns fiercely on the dream's edge.
Clipper ships burst into ten-story flames
on a night-locked ocean vanishing back
behind things that appear here, where we are.

A small song of Shakespeare's now survives this,
the basement scent let go back into grief
for the lovers who, leaving, still share love,
for the fool who has sobered still singing,
for the aging that keeps us from loving, for

thickening that locks us in our ways.
Armor at the bottom of the ocean
dimly glows, encrusted, as we forget.
Birch pages stack up on the rain's table.

FRACTIONS LIT BY SUN

I.

People who had believed in the color *green*,
ocean waves sending once their feeding rains,
the gorge falls behind
atomic tedium expelling
long afternoon over this fraction
through all dark blast flash not happening,

the planetary crux in the crucible of kindness,
through thumping chest-swims breath knows
the beginning of, something like a dissolved room
where a white door frame empties into a pasture,
where two people went mid day
small flowers burning in future cells.

II.

What doesn't happen takes away more than
we know, the single revolution through
convergence in a moment of time,
the mists from grasshoppers, from under the lift
and fall of milk from the breast of the moon,
from inside the question
and its answer,
beauty – the counter-clockwise stirred
by the clockwise, the primordialized sparks
wheeling under your microscope,
where spinal candles
curve with slippery bodily slopes,
the build up neighborhoods grated into parts
of ground, a woman just having gone

through an iron gate. Somewhere an ancestor
is making her shoes
in morning spin, light
having turned when.

III.

Ocean fish drift through tinctures
spreading in the mouth of the soaked river,
factories constructed around furnaces
of hope where air is scat-blasted
back into first air, the chartreuse
games given off by completion
and the long giving sunlight has
as our Earth-scaffolding
passing through roundingness-color,

the beered-up out shouting, the squealing
(even in little) shrill religious massive cross
Ferris wheel dipping them down under,
yet something like a white door
opening at the top of time, the post-war melting
ice a crystal carpet off-draining, the liminal
imperative of sudden ripe sliced oranges
a missed note broken over and over its protons,
that squeak of Keds on the varnished wooden floor

where childhood moved, the close hello
through grasping of the baby's hand,
where a stairway went right up
into blank night between generations.

IV.
Solar wind picked up
by a boy whose body
had formed his thinking
carried him further
than someone might have known
listening to the static,

the solar energy exquisite, the tropical bell
sound inside us from neutrinos,
the mother that rain is
with bees that tend

to enter flowers as if they loved
them, the boy old enough
to regard the young
woman not far from him
as if he could someday
be someone kind beside her.

V.
Someone who has listened to bees old enough,
old enough, some people not even understanding
being this old, the flower stalks
reaching ahead of a body, the hypnotic numerals
stone after stone back toward the horizon,

at the stroke of daylight in necks of squirrels,
summer wind that propels the curve of snails,
the black box magnetic fields sending the young off,
where from behind his mask a worker felt his face
in this market, sensing the rolling of ground

into violet shadows of a distant mountain,
where hours before the military jeeps had passed
and a man had spoken to the woman
as if he knew her and would return.

GOING ON BEFORE GOING

Don't the animals cry and sing under the moon
and sun, lowing and bellowing, roaring, thumping,
calling, chuckling, using their sense and voices?
When you're flat on your back, will you drink
through a glass straw? Do you favor resuscitation
by extraordinary means? What day of the week
was yesterday? Whose coup took the government?
Don't the cells choose? Isn't the body thinking,
in all the cells and systems they have in place alive?

May the mind grow quiet, calmer than the silence
after elephantine thunders have contacted others
in their tribe. What's everything you might want
or need when it's gone? What's anything that's yours
if the risks are resting on others? May better sense
overtake the place fast. May what must be shared
by everyone alive be claimed by beings in perpetuity.

Could what's gone be going on, crowding in tight
while vanishing? What day does it happen to be
when who knows where the time goes in its old car?
May the chief end of people help lessen suffering
of others. May education end, but not before dying.

FREEFALL

I.

As if there were a beautiful, terrifying, extra-dimensional entity,

as if it were an extrapolation of the beautiful and terrifying nature

of the planet, when so many systems at once now are producing,

II.

interacting, simultaneously creating an extraordinarily complex

need for words in a universe much more vast, we can see now

from the Hubble, than what we learned back where each of us was

III.

growing up, how the mind has continued to fill in, supplying faces,

colors, even the locations where a God beyond us would be found,

as if when it's sleeping, the brain will be cooking up more nature

IV.

for its resume of symbols, dependent as they are on constellations

of neurological collaboration, where the government of the brain

must invest its trust in a cabinet usually somewhere on this planet

V.

of water and earth, where the job of music is telling us more how

to live: and yet where is the ground-breaking human evolutionary

moratorium on war, whatever kind, you name it, or on being crazy

VI.

about battlefield sales, as if fighting originated with personal meals

given to meat-eating, centuries of digesting chopped animal muscle,

as if people were fighting an endless war to end their mutual needs?

REMAINS OF THE LAST NAME

Resistance breaks with tradition by stopping compliance with
present conditions always being focused

on the unfinished future   street-carried flat and round
as your last name

                          in the voice of a friend beginning again
    the ascent sound makes knowing oceanic cells have gone sunlit in
        surprising builds of chords through which we've turned out of
        evolution to the purposes of longing,

    where we've all been one another one way or another
                          moving quickly or slowly, like the morning.

        For every old possibly forgotten marrow in bone
    buried in desire has always been connected
                through parts of the whole indigenous to its make-up

that stands with every redwood and bullfrog's primordial singing

                    where the mammalian afternoon has had its people
    speaking serious species tongue, the way it is
        being any animal lit from within the reception of sun
    in cells where it started   into hatchings and births

down streaming cords   to deliver us   each one
    fit for self-repairs and diva dives, tanning and being paid in salts

no matter the flux or what flow of the indigo-ultraviolet unknown advances
                while receding from how it grows lovely,
        orderly and wildly tropospheric   as the last rains steam

when a hummingbird takes to the air
    without trying, as easily
as gravity holds boulders down   at the bottom of water forming rivers
    that flow through being.

15

REMAINS OF BEING AWAKE

Since what you're thinking comes from you
    and someplace other that reaches you in time

  therefore, what you're thinking is yours and yet not yours, with
  wind-slid Arabic numerals off the sky charts

  indicating galaxies on all sides of fairly uncertain consequences
      arranging nevertheless for a necklace

       to be worn around beauty
       of the original forests
       where intelligence has been
 honest as the next ethics still emerging
         around blank-slate
       requests for sudden reassurance.

As maps exist in the inherited speech of your father
  and mother, it's good to listen, to rule out
    false assumptions placed on the steel tables
     with first merging lost and required attempts

       to breathe all at once around
   spiral towers elevated mystically electric with
  mushrooming past felt foundational kinesis

as reconstructs the fall forestry of courage with surges
    in procreative safe passage more integrated the
  more we're able to hoist propellers
from the old volumes into winds, from the invisible to the seen.

ON THE LOOSE

Epidemiologists said shutting down the economy could save 1 to 2
million lives. So 1 million lives saved at $10 million each, that's $10
trillion. That's about half of the U.S. GDP in a year.
                    – **NPR, on** *All Things Considered*

Irreversible births collect. A new human appears,
undertaking the first steps over a good half
of the antiquated declarations inscribed in
stone by chiselers working with what they saw
as theirs on behalf of the crown
or energy at the maw in redemption.

If no choices remain within stone-serious gravitas
that crashes through architecture, the ancestors
were spot-wrong about mystery spilling ships
off the edges of Earth, and wrong about peopling
the Earth as our destiny and not something
so hungry we serve its every whim,
if only to stop it from consuming us.

With sirens on Eisenhower highways in capitalism,
invisible fixes on human value and alarm clocks,
synaptic veils between the unconscious and conscious
reaching out of a Jeffersonian sea-orchid cultural
innocence impossible to write down, where instinct is

behind the telephoto third eye, watching for the chalice
of mindfulness, the grail of common good pouring down
blue sky, racking up indebtedness, living in US dollars,
maybe a way to determine human value
in US dollars is to lock a few greedier

billionaires on death row to learn
what their fixers offer to get them off.
No one else could possibly
afford the astronomical price.

REMAINS ON THE PLANETARY SURFACE

I. Red Howlers at Dusk

Let no time passing fail the test
   of unusual luck   trickling down on the clock

 for the love of companions
   where we've started out small,
  close to the ground, which is the case

for anything made out of cells   so you don't have far to fall
if you're trying to get both legs to collaborate

    to carry weight in one direction then the other.

Where the old disciplines convene in a spectrographic spike

that causes red howlers to grin before crying out in their howl
from the shock of consciousness,

      in the only solar dusk
    when light's on fire between the poles,

   there's fire beyond, bearing this heaviness
     as global rain falls in cells,
 fire on ghost-talked proving grounds
  as humbleness faces gargantuan forces,

    when there's gravity to get a grip on.

Whatever raised us before we could think has left us with scripts.

Let us recall how it felt to be in swoons of love,
    when wrestling fear in the void
until loving each part of what have you,

    as Earth rises over the lunar horizon.

II. Blue We Can See

Out of respect for common birth, all people

                        understand hungers

          caused by revolving in orbit around the sun,

                 where there's enough to go around

   for sunlight to draw on experience, which draws experience out,

as if altruism were the real price of admission

that exempts no one.

                 And yet as we are, we live as someone

       interrelated with similar others, each one

    in a similar life so different nothing could take it out of us.

The green plants reminding us of the niche we inherited

in the ecosystem for which the head was developed

an unthinkably long time ago by the cells.

    Then we imprinted on what we found with our senses

      when we were little, the first times we had the chance

   to look around, down at the dirt

   or up into the afternoon cooked up in leaves.

Hearing the smallest chime, inhaling it   with the scent of juniper,

   we saw what we could feel and see.

                  The blue couldn't have been

higher, which had us hoping   solar vibration making things hum.

III. Sidewalk Violin

For breath to become breath,
with the body inextricably ignited,
                         individuated but part of living unity,
matter pivots on unpulled fast inclinations of the genome
that over the leguminous time
overflow.
                         For hunger begins somewhere out of sight,

liquid light, dark as breathing,
growing calm around everyone home.

Look – drop your arsenal
    at the foot of the Sphinx
                              which remains toothless
around those who thirst at the fountain of peace keeping them alive.

A long precipitous fall lifts off the wild seas

    as weight sinks in rain   toward the pavilion of lions,

if you have a mind to employ bioluminescence
making your path through miles of solitude,

if you walk in your own footsteps simultaneously particle and wave
intact in your clockwork
going off where you go,

                    while someone standing by the glass bus stop
                                        plays sidewalk violin
    in pursuit of moss-glowing green   going on plumb

    as it is written   in a script of bee-turns.

IV. These Conditions

It's possible a species as aggressive as ours
                    will survive wars between its nation-states
         and the brutality passed along one generation to the next

                             unless a new war turns thermonuclear.

What the species won't survive is its all-out assault on ecosystems.

The way the body evolves in response to conditions,

              in increments that refine what's been put in place,
                   the conditions we need around us evolve

based on forces and locations of matter with effects of combustion,

         releases of gasses, loss of species to drought or flooding,
   bursts of volcanoes or missile bombardment, loss of the usual
     global circulation of cooling or warming currents of air or water.

So extraordinary heat stays with carbon molecules in the atmosphere,

heat that penetrates whatever the air touches with conductivity
                    starting with water, causing oceans to bake
                    slowly, almost from the inside out.

    The longer politics stops the collective from acting en masse

    as fast as possible to replace equipment and practices
    that lead to the blood boiling,

    when food stops growing,
                         the more it will cost everyone alive
                         and the harder the end will hit.

V. Tuesday Evening

So the hermetic arts have invested in under-accommodated senses.
Solar showers have left deserted shade where the moth's disappeared.

Minutia have been promoted as fundamental to stinking childhood.

Sun has darkened us bright when we were old or quite young.
Concentration of the mind remains a live emanation of the cells.

It's hard enough, never been easy   to live as a being
                                        human with humane beliefs
          able to base differences   on what's in common.
     No one among us exists who never went through birth.
     No one has a mind able to survive without the plants.

We're so close we could miss it, too hung up on differences

     to consider the possible practice of peace
               to stop trying to please the sheriff in hankering,
                    the diminished fifth in the horn player,

     the physician who held your head shortly following birth,
     the reverend who preached into an unfathomable bucket,

as if you've never stopped answering   the impractical test
when you're seeing inscrutable faces   of human aspiration

          where inexorable flowerhead lift has its yearning
          at moth speeds,   so great an urgency exists.

II.

To stop the flow of music would be like the stopping
of time itself, incredible and inconceivable.
- Aaron Copland

It's after the end of the world.
- Sun Ra

UNCERTAINTY

The polar ice cap melts, polar bears drown or wander
down to garbage bins, while polarization spreads
through the North American family. What began in the '60s
as a credibility gap has transformed and regrouped
over time becoming a gulf, and now is a swamp from before
the original Jesus zeroed out the years, a thick swamp
of impenetrable orientations, forget about the Orient,
forget about bioluminescent sunset others call *dawn*,
as intercontinental ballistic policies call themselves meals,
referring Jeffersonian liberal education to a specialist
in esemplastic surgery for the slightest blood irregularity.

The glassy-eyed Pomeranian may be quick but isn't sure
who to believe about going outside. One camp pursues policy
while the other demands power, using tactics of the first grade
playground handbook. The TV show of startling sensation
in the will to power throws a real tantrum, for domination
over facts, then reveals a happy woman beside a happy man
whose stream has widened. Mammoth unfamiliar spiraling
storms blow sideways across the gulf. There're indications
of north and south, down and up, long and quick, newly hired
or lowered—the Civil War Confederacy perks up, awash
with supremacy, attacking others' health care, undertaking
enormous business as if fighting a war. On the nearby shore
are people living in 1950s towns, at the edge of the 1870s
prairies, where a redwood picnic table of seriously intent
cheerleaders and night guards entertains the idea of 2040.

CUT OF THE BLADE

The moon's unfinished arc which floats
like a Moroccan blade over the cornfield
won't show much of what is going on
in the slowly evolving conscious mind.
The equator, all the while, races around
with unthinkable ancestry, as the mostly
unseen poles hold onto wheeling space.

Streetlights continue drowning out stars
in their electrical magnetic flow and flux
over ongoing stretches, as they continue
to throw down salmon shadows darkening
the spectrum as it prisms into conditions,
leaving a ruin of bleached coral in regret.

It turns out the sea of uncountable tankers
can ruin the pulse down in a violet eyelash,
in a flash of legal maneuvering. In 2007,
the worth of a human being live was set
by actuarial councils around $6.9 million
by experts with much experience in the area.

Mammoth consequences fly in a phalanx
of brown pelicans. A Hawaiian rain mists
into silent yards of diffuse conscious mind
still in construction. Lit with questioning,
indigenous South American calendars wheel
within mathematical groves where ancient
hungers were guided by the remarkable bees.

MUSCLED OFF THE PLANE

A mooling trek in a velvet ball gown unbridled by innocence.

A mint-shut leaf-over of Bavarian warrior royalty in an elk rut.

A mother among us with a firm grip on the upturned hull.

A white dog with balding white eyes of trans-Arctic melting.

An eschatological belief unsnapping leathers down to torturous
    meaninglessness pouring off the human trunk in a flood
    of root-combed bone-making that drives the air ahead.

An unequal distribution where nobody's watching, if not dancing
    for the quickly damned adumbrations of us.

A goose-necked train station sawing mammoth guillotine drops
    into beautiful bones of distantly stranded sea birds.

A few system failures that cause suffering, but for only a while
    with dungeonous severance on the downslope of oil.

A few fresh pallets of culturally activated incendiary devices
    aching over the years as if something definitive should be done
    to stop the deaths of the animals.

A leftover of hundreds of tons a second factory-floor machinery
    in NASA booster assembly plants here in the primal cauldron.

A trio of gospel women swaying to radical shammering tambourine
    stops and starts, in their luminous ultramarine satin robes.

A blond burst stealing away where the means of production are
    finally returned to local hands around public
    re-enactments of angry men impervious to front-line
    questioning next door to your own prehistoric undoing.

With another's top-down rural electrification of the gargantuan
    up-mothered machine of berserk overseas war
    outlined in bold Rouault fanning out in undertow.

A thinly veiled onyx-scarlet rock muscling the self ahead of light.

A demonstration of cells that eventually assembled into neo-cortex
    around R-complex with courageous longing

at the time of cellular birth, waging the impossible
through discontent that unfrocks and swipes its blade.
A sleep-bewrenched silence nailed down by roadside motel neon.
With a fresh spike of externalized heat, contemplative and bawdy
    from an unfinished future squeezing mammoth bellows
    of unusual psychic beauty and harshness forced
    onto colt-thick attempts not to vanish in our time.

THE JOB OF PHARAOH

When you consider that the position of being Pharaoh
required the person to sit with an elevated attitude
for hours in a gold gargantuan chair on a platform
at a height where he could see everyone in the room
in the Pharaonic throne hall, where he sat but soared
over aqueducts and tropical canopies as he watched over
domiciles and common quarters, scrutinized the borders
with an eye on the calendar, while managing transversal
oppositions of sun and moon, you might ask how he sat
so long without breaking out of rank to raid the kitchen
or head out with a score of posthypnotic bathing women
and men who were ballfield comrades with a good sense
of humor and regard for the latest improvisatory bands
with an intellectual edge and infectious drum-beat urge.

The point may have been for the sitting Pharaoh to actualize
each moment by making it a breakthrough of embodiment,
to occupy the center of civilization toward which the stars
are pointing out of cosmic arrangement that exacerbates
power of each knife, leverage of laboring musclemen, draw
of a dancer's hand turning, and so forth. In this way, a man
fulfilling his purposes could rest assured, without fearing
the fall of his own shadow if it loomed large on a stone wall.
Maybe he'd say to a buddy, "I don't know about your plan
or understand your methods, but I know the Pharaoh sits
on the throne of what we know, that order reigns over all."

THE DIVINE

As the traveler who has lost his way throws his reins on the horse's
neck and trusts to the instinct of the animal to find his road, so must
we do with the divine animal who carries us through the world.
– R.W. Emerson

If the gold-faced sitting Pharaoh is divine,
so are the multitudes of bathing women
with whom the Pharaoh's power consorts.
This includes each priest with a mouthful,
each weaver of cane webbing on a chair back,
as well as each organic capillary delivery
of what becomes a sip of the Pharaoh's water
accepted from an Earth-jeweled divine vessel
created by communal artisans of the court,

folks who studied athletically with divine Magi
belonging to schools of the cosmic callosum,
back when bearded professors divined answers.
Of course, delivering their work at conferences
forced them into long journeys in caravans
of humans on backs of animals that descended
with people from the first organic individuals,

where if the Pharaoh's divine, it would be a trait
shared by the stock he comes from, the animals
that accompany people on journeys sometimes
through hostile territory, but on ground familiar
to humpbacked camels and local donkeys on firm
footing with matter, in accord with differentiation
of human and donkey, the bovine and avian, labor
and executive faculties, tropical and polar divine,

where who isn't made out of a lot that has been,
is, and will be off the clock when on it, at the heart
of the matter, the maker and tool, the wooden flute
and remote ancestors of the musician letting it
resonate for the mother and child, for the father
and stallion with the colt, the Pharaoh and child,
for the milk cows grazing in the reach of people,
as the divine animal carries us through the world?

THE QUEEN JOINS THE BANQUET

The Queen of Sheba enters the banquet hall
in which regional family and tribal heads
and bone-reading philosophers have gathered.
In her emerald-studded headdress of white ibis feathers
and rhino horn, the queen appears to be floating,
as if the underground itself were kneeling in supplication
to what's above. Lingering on the way into the hall,
the queen shimmers, golden brown, bathing in radiance
of a huge stone hearth in which whole forest trunks burn.
The path before her opens naturally, as was prophesied.
As above, therefore below. The queen's face of kindness
lifts if she happens to move. The royal procession instantly
threads the needle eye, delivering her to her rightful position
in the room, in mother territory, which is inevitable.
As people gaze at her, it appears the queen's not aging.
Therefore, the planted fields and sacred womb remain
fertile. After devotional singing, it's time for evening repast.
Through her high priestesses, the queen gives the sign
for concentrated silence, then for public eating to commence.
On great elongated *Afrocarpus gracilior* tables hand-carved
with lion, hippo, baboon, roots of climbing green plants
and the history of waters, are cured meats of species
from across the land on fine platters. An hour is a minute,
a flash over fifty years, an avalanche of generations.
The Queen of Sheba walks, floating into the 19th century
mansion of an industrialist to sit at the great table
of archaic assumptions, that those born elevated stand
over what's below. Her royal presence remains
to be inherited by descendants and persists
until, desperately outmoded, it's overthrown.

ONWARD BUSINESS SOLDIERS

After they'd had at the indigenous,
they set upon the endogenous.
They offered never-before-seen chemistry
with a will unbridled by consequences.
They stumped the masses by selling them
on what they hadn't noticed
were their definitive ailments.
For lubricating parts of the mechanical
19th century body, they held up
alcohol mixed with oil of the snake.
They demonstrated a concerted interest
in destroying forests one tree at a time.
They labeled the collected sum of bottom lines
the economy, running it up the flagpole.
They employed divisions of the public
relations crowd who banked on the importance
of stupendous goods, to bypass reason
and sink pseudo-Freudian roots in stupidity.
They unstudied what they were fed in school
from the earliest feed-lot appearance
busting with pride over the defeat of nature.
They grabbed chaos by the tiger tornado
to parcel it out on the know-all market
using locomotive steam-driven ditch-digging rigs,
gold compasses, and unbending T-squares.
They came marching out of Europe and firing,
before sitting on a tinder box of denial
and assumed exceptionalism: they couldn't stop
extending their reach through every port
across every spread they could possibly claim.

PURITAN MATTERS

Among these would be [1] utter concentration
on the father, particularly the invisible father,
[2] risking the lives of their loved ones to pursue
an imaginary world, [3] picking an imaginary
world already packed with archaic presences
that later would require mammoth public denial,

[4] sinking the taproot of private joy into an absolute
future subjugation of insects in the surroundings,

[5] digging further than seven feet down to bury desire
with lust and objects of aesthetic appeal or superstition,

[6] allowing unaddressed matters buried to fester
below, until they flared up in endless caverns
of flame boiling transgressors in red-black hell fire,

[7] causing research and intensified development
of a portable instant sense of personal rejection
the psyche carries, [8] elevating stature of public
execution sanctioned by old Western conventions,
then inversely worshiping it,

               [9] kneeling humbly
to wrestle dark death into the strictly knowable,
when [10] ostracizing the irrepressible drummers
and graceful dancers, [11] banking on the opposite
of embodied time at the expense of others trying to live,

[12] initiating the harsh removal of what's been
incomplete, while [13] remembering the script
and yet forgetting the play, [14] preparing the town
square to fit all, after crossing lines, crafting stocks
and bonds to exact measures of biblical torture.

                    Impossible to overlook would be
[15] relegating play to the realms of small children,
while [16] finding young idle hands intolerable,

[17] discovering a land where people were living
openly but seeing it as the devil's playground,
[18] enduring sufferings of self and others
close to them but hardening further, [19] failing

to practice more traditional musical instruments
other than for worshiping the unseen father
believed to always be angry about wickedness,

[20] judging smallest acts to be mean, meaningless,
unless they did bidding of the overseeing father,

[21] witnessing beauty of women in front of them
but requiring they don darkened robes drawn shut,

[22] closing the back room so squealing hungry
children could be quieted by women, or else,

[23] taking what may have been pleasing or vivid,
even pleasurable, as an unspent fuel of misdeeds,

[24] causing women to speak for kids in the world
of adult agony and disregard, [25] shattering
the vulnerable back of the fugue on the anvil
of unison, when [26] believing in almighty fear,
thinking the survival of everyone depends on it.

Unforgotten are [27] infiltrating from supernumerary
tintype images of long-bearded great grandfathers
who muscled plows behind their Trojan work horses,

[28] developing abominable means of recollection
and commencement of lone begging for blanket
forgiveness, while [29] allowing ancient shadows
of death to live again through martyrdom believed
capable of causing magical transmutations,

[30] lynching the horses to present powers of death,
[31] then teaching this to people still alive
as their absolute future hinged on obedience.

A FOUNDING FATHER OF THE NRA EXPRESSES HEARTFELT ADMIRATION

Billy—you always shows how tough you is,
    which is all anyone out here got
    onct they's clum plumb off they's settle

and moseyed round they's hot hors, with every
    damn one out for hisself, but you juss
    step up, Kid, showing where you gonna go

without Jesus Christ nobody here holdin you
    back, throwing you down, or kickin
    lights out of you, but everyone stand back

like they's seein some ghost in the dust, as you step
    where you want, nobody knowin you good
    or bad on your draw, as you got the quickest

finger and you's got your stranger standin there
    asking for it, what you brung with you,
    to shut they trap like they oughta and juss

stand back to admire your walk, as history's bunk
    and nobody need more fool book learnin
    when the light's goin dark for anyone movin

wrong or bawlin crazy as a buffalo widow or flappin
    they's tongue like it don't never stop—but
    you show 'em, Billy, how it done god damn it.

THE TIME OF A FEW GARGANTUAN NEST EGGS

There is no trickle down, only a siphoning up from the toiling many to the moneyed few.
— **Michael Parenti**

The blood sports of billionaire money-mongers leaving 100s
       of 1000s' homelessness unanswered.
The wisdom of an army of money traveling on a few thin dimes
       of the masses who have no choice.
The safety in having so much money in vaults no one would know
       how to spend it, unless she's a billionaire.
The security in possessing money so heavy none of the serving
       persons could carry it off. Period.
The beauty of astronomical numbers of bucks siphoned up
       from everyone else under midnight stars.
The astonishing contributions of computerization to laundering
       unbridled billionaire campaign investment.
The lunacy around religiously owning so much no one can tell
       if your image proves you're a god.
The difficulty of forbidding rank trespassers on your newly
       and suddenly privatized public lots.
The one billion that spawns millions without doing anything or
       being touched by anyone else.
The immaculate conception with billionaire parthenogenesis
       absent the local community.
The problem of the Constitution not establishing hoarding rights
       of monomaniacal money-mongers.
The insurmountable burden of urgency in the craven desire to
       collect astronomically huge money.
The upside-down world as billionaires take credit for efforts
       of the managers and serving persons.

The lethal involuntary money-mongering instantaneously at war
        against human-with-human cooperation.
The archaic ritual of primordial reckonings having a field day
        with the needy who remain anonymous.
The paleoconservatives in their liberty behind razor wire and armed
        guard towers smoking familial stogies.
The molecular impression of providence buoyant on the sea
        of symbiotic mostly unnamed microorganisms.
The disembodied distortions that bargain for cut-throat executions
        of the market in invisibility.
The gargantuan money-hoarding which endures chronic suffering
        of others without having to trouble itself.
The rancid spikes of leachate and drool that trickle down off the lip
        of wealth's landfills dripping into watersheds.
The cherubic rich cabinet permanently pressed for want of Central
        Intelligence getting when the getting's good.
The ease with which money flows and splashes over rocks and
        talks louder than one person thinking.
The innocent coal miners sweetly perishable in downhill slides
        of money melting until veins collapse.
The fluffed-up agenda of wealth contingent on the invisible hand
        of transnational exhortations.

BOTTLENECK

At the blazing entrance to eternity,
the long build-up of societal bulk
would still be sporting Egyptian dinner
jackets and fox-body stoles alongside
accessorized raingear with subArctic
mufflers and Philippine guard belts,
black and yellow contemporary racing
shoes, pilgrim-buckle grandma's galoshes,
and pointy-toed hard-nailed tango heels
all throwing their weight into instinctive

attempts to simultaneously transact
at the baroque transom before entering
the great superconscious choral halls.
But we're at least a generation and a half
behind these days in shoulder-to-shoulder
compression at the quasi-spatial edges
of timelessness, given the whole number
of recently departed souls with good enough
global intentions nevertheless throwing
sharp unintended elbows into Sicilian ribs,

backing steel cart rims into quartermaster
shins, chickeny kneecaps jabbing swollen
calves, where the decks have been mixed
then stacked, minus the jokers and certain
royal families, everyone milling around
on cloud barges, with numbers lugging in
euphonium or bass-clarinet cases as rock

into slight and oily string-handled shop bags
bearing fast-trucked interstate grapefruit
or violet knit snowflake mittens for seriously

anticipated grandchildren. It's one individual
at a time floating in from a snapped fuselage
or undisclosed riparian territory, only one
a time, who wears a nude Parisian hair net
or yellow-orange hard hat, or aquamarine
looped velveteen ribbon, reaching the lobby
where individuals are telling of transitional
late experiences in 7th floor business English,
Latvian, making heavy breath in Argentinian
script, Jesuit Latin, vocal Kiowa accompanied

by ritual drum, up there in the whispered din,
as assumptions turn belief out in ten thousand
directions, after surfacing from salt-sea swells
off the Iberian Peninsula, or from a heated-up
mating retreat behind barn-wood Dutch doors
in a Miami plaza, or off the gold-trimmed eaves
of a Cambodian jungle temple, or having fallen
through crisp Olympic rings of hand-rubbed
meditation skulls, where the center of mass
congestion exists within everyone who waits.

III.

When you swim you don't grab onto the water.
- **Alan Watts**

One way to open your eyes is to ask yourself,
"What if I had never seen this before?
What if I knew I would never see it again?
- **Rachel Carson**

SMOLDERING WING-BEAT SWELLS

I.

The well-oiled condescension behind flood-lit razor wire
prehistory along back-lit edges of the next rain falling to Earth
the blood-seeing circumstances embraced through a feather

the planet's core that spins on what's made the body round

the current blossoming plum and yellow bamboo skirts seen here
in the future collective where centuries go down unremembered
fast into root-cooled animal-shouldered antiquity, in archaic states

of fluorescence, for nothing exists when nothing exists but what's here

the half-cry of the dog peppering the boneyard while the tundra thaws
releasing more atmospheric gasses, more tied to what hopes in a molecule
where the first breath burns through the whole continuing to flame

in the afternoon the tall drink of water encyclopedic with untested hungers

the amber-gold fertility and versatility invested in an old forest necklace
the current silence as designates conscious borders of working days

with overpopulations, a little wealth, and far more impoverishment
and medieval impregnations arcing over bone-down arisings of gravity
in the rain that falls steadily losing its animals to the difficult miles
of sublime last principles of the wilderness probably not in your language
or your political architecture, where 18th-century assumptions are still
taking it out on the commons like nobody's business, in long moves
of synaptic operations on Celsius from drivers' seats of unknowing

cardboard shacks mushrooming from muds at the outskirts, multiply
projected electrical current in flashes of blood-ties between animals.

II.

The magnetic absence or presence of bees working the perimeter
the shock of hips caught in the soundless ring of Ice Age bells

as the sun branches into almonds and shade through the root roar

the thundering multiple aortic regenerations rippling along transpolar
arcs in the complexity of fresh water that falls in the spectrum of being

the look a hawk gives a shining silver sedan before they both take off
the canary singing the overhead sun higher and to beautiful canaries
a reddened-brown translucent flicker hammering on a ripe fir trunk

hawks circling through a loose thermal, the hundreds of years that pass

each day pouring through cathedrals of wind, the descending appetites
foraging through all the blinding blue blazes behind red-scarlet curtains

in the embassy of opposites, in the inflation of global rain as feathers off

historic melts in the saucering galaxy, with furious 2nd-century faults
where you may have been well owned or saved by surgical polarization

of tribes encircled, where tongues touch as other animals, before words

before the absentee fish-flop of unconditional doubt had been slammed
onto one of the steel tables in standing overflow of present contractions
of the bearings steaming and withheld from our fathers' *Book of Intent*

the soot of China, which has carried across rising oceans of language
where Detroit ants colonize branches of intuited raw oceanic wages

where rain's unable to stop falling and the ocean keeps farming us out
from before words into self, where identity pitches a tent in the overhead
blue with iridescent scarlet squid at unknown depths, sea stars locked
into rock of the coast, however intuitive or encrusted the carnivorous

up-roiled murk is when it surrenders to serious flux in all fierce lift

or spool that turns in splits, the zero-cry death may be as rejoinings
stop, growing cold, however much may be breathing in mineral cells

with seawater screen doors that slam out of principle, discovering
the molten core of biological necessity emptying to again be filled.

III.

The kindness and sad cases vaporizing in a quick walk to the car
the arcing draw of integers and brown-rice taste of stored sunlight

the gyres of cellular knowledge transacting swift cross-pollination

the hourly newborn interweaving within sense, the waking in faces

with splashes of corn, the electromagnetized up-swayed polar encircling
protoplastic Amazon stretches going past diurnally launched liminal sides

the further means of breakthrough of body where matter has its ends

on ground floors of subdimensions in rations of sunlight's caressing
from a long way back, from the future of black-crimson ribs of dog stars
the socioeconomic Big Dippers wielded by the distracted or reabsorbed

the genetic conventions from mammal mothers of mothers in a crack
of another eggshell sentence no longer, from before star-necked general
dispensations beholden to the vulnerable, as to a little horse-cart current

boiler-making public trust, the antiquity of uncountable acts peopling
the place, the arcing draw along a few thumbprints of vanishing sky

swells of oceanic Stravinsky before owl-purred half-absolute floods

tanagers that call from within the tanager they've continued to talk
the brain that pursues sleep in a bed which cradles what it becomes
the earliest mammal shaking muds from fur of the species, the beauty
that shows what a species has learned, as the mineral Earth turns

into a feather, the moment in which being someone's the same being
for all species, the same global entanglement, the larger seen to a tiniest

root imperative of topsoil in which uncounted colonies are keeping us
alive in differing stories than drumhead unison, than accumulating vaults
of spoils of chemistry and striving that once comforted us, the buoyancy

that draws sunlight out of the air with its body-to-body engravings.

IV.

The alternative currents with enough cargo to refill eyesight, to send
clocks reeling on their cables carrying out unheard-of live broadcasts

of news which rewrite inherited assumptions, the rare tusks aimed
at earnestness in uniform folds you could have lived with between lives
once the whole waking within the brain decides it would rather not sleep

before newly grown stops and starts as are sound, blue concentrations

rising with tide, the chickadee threading between what cannot be taken

back by anonymity, the crimson burn that settles down in a nutshell

in articulated amber licks of Charlie Parker at the origin of golden horn

as processions transmogrify suddenness making their own boilerplate

royal chime, their own means of saying *yes* or *no* that the sea otter

or whole marigold seems like us, the mothering old dust with cellular

volts in a wing beat, the membranous swallows of indefinite passing

holds at the edges of this era where charred sails have still been heading

to not, or an opposite morphed into postocular setae and denatured corn

which serves purposes imposed more than selected, that stands between

the naked human back and the fire, in the rock of the next to the next

as reverberates in weight-bearing sacrament, in the spontaneous televised

galaxy before the wall of Greenland suggestion, the ends of ice melting

in the middle of anyone live, the past filling or emptying of '50s facsimiles

of the microsecond, with terrific splits scraping nail tips on pre-emphatic

meaning and anyone's benign attempts behind parasympathetic ancestry

to align tissue with bone, lanterning the quick ants' truck from sleep

into waking where generations rest within smoldering wing-beat swells.

V.

With construction and collapse mostly from nowhere each moment

we cannot waste, root winds sweep out of the nuclear space in forgotten

capacity, as intuited further generations fly in raw, the ocean farming us

51

out into self where identity pitches a tent, surrendering to serious flux

out of down-bent regard, before black-box election steals far from united
in the liquid propensity, driven by everything they're part of or close to

moving through doors at the root of swimming cells, the circling billions
of suns, millions of beliefs, the ten thousand sins and any peak experience
grandfathered in, orbiting where momentum's the work of future light
the disciplines with spear-tip readiness that bolsters the historical present
the ethical collaboration on intricate means to the ends we've embraced

the way time goes when no one should be denied the means of survival

where flux flows along strings, formless and formed, in the flush of stark
eggshell atmosphere, the sad heads on mammalian necks, the great aunts
at funerals of species, grieving loss of the future in silence, the inevitable

conquest of one fragment of dust over another, the ambulation of cells
which started in ocean pools of the first world where cells in their swims
have gone bioluminous in how much time could it be through the culls

and starts of heat cycles stuck in old-time belief with its elemental burns

of gut-rumbling glistering industrial hunger to acquire night then sell it
back even to night, the pearl-clustered lays of egg under the sky's million
billions, contingent plants fired up in binges, in light of the long tradition

of civilized yields and half-eaten scenes of Bosch bristling with crawls
where the new world could never end in terpsichorean sluice in future

converging Celsius at work on the current Anthropocene Era of day.

VI.

The original solar predilections, genetic Pythagoras and Dali
the medicine skeleton and rare birth you were ready to inhabit

the coyote circling back behind languages of other species

the filtering bioswales in psyche, the ladling spiral genome

Bartok shadow thrown onto homes with flames of magnetic wind

Bach within evolution of a multiple-chorded womb-walled fetus
the falling lift that fills the simple rounding-off of a Fuji apple
the sea-level lightning as accompanies anyone's surviving chance

the night into which each day comes from surviving edges that roar
a forest of lumens in cells, that quicken what they hold in readiness

and sacrifice that grieves without notice, that tenders necks of violas
and germinates quickness for rash tresses and rock within cells

in the night apples held close to the sternum of orchard branch.

WESTERN MATTER AND ENERGY

The angle of personal torque is the spine
    of delivered power. After much
of the matter engages then uncouples,
    it can slide around core as a wave
of solar gamma rays unfolds, delivering
    mathematical particles in quantum
probability through light that breaks down
    over matter working uncertainty alive
where belief takes questions and finds itself
    maybe more honest. In the torque of light,
blood-hot with up-or-down votes, the dusk
    of rifled herds has already been here
back-blasting and lost in Manifest Destiny,
    opening up from Pullman whiskey cars
being hauled around by vast locomotives
    of endless Earth, it must have been,
close enough to shoot clean through hearts
    of the herd from their car seats.
As the boys aimed Remingtons at buffalo,
    not many of them were thinking
they were escaping the father and god
    of the fathers, as they cracked out
rounds at the bawling place they'd found
    where no one cares. And they knew
the place—vast, enough to make them rich,
    so whatever they did, nothing they'd do
would harm it, how it's inhaling locomotive
    smoke with roaring buffalo whippings,
pumping a horse alive in each man's chest.
    The red and black primordial future

and past will go down to their heat, with gun
	powder blistering the scent they have
teaching children respect, and how to take
	what they need. On a Wednesday,
the conifers fly past hearses as leaves sink
	their root to the core, and we're here,
reconfiguring survival this time everything
	will be understood for the energy
it takes or whips up, generates or shaves.

HUNGER TURNS HEAVY

The brain entertains the mind
with inlaid Mediterranean tile.
Would this be a place where nothing is
photoshopped? Maybe you can help me.
Can you direct me to your leader?
I've come from a different planet than the one
we're seeing now. Multiplicity this instant
settles in with dead-bolt accuracy somewhere
in the gut. Words will not set us apart
from everything breathing, the other species
with which we've evolved. Common explanations
no longer hold. One note to the next goes by
the wind and spine. Evolving pteropods echo
one another. Shirtless boys still swim in the ocean
of afternoon sunlight on the ball field of 1959.
The neural net has been cast in the long story
of yields. Shadow splashes up with the spectrum.
Before it ends, the road goes on. It goes off
on its own accord. Winds roll through
the species, while the foghorn resounds,
moaning out of the unconscious bay.

STEAMING FIELDS

The souped or rash steaming rise of multiple Jesus,
the rock of Brazilian canopy as central rain goes out,
the erogenous receptivity taking the unfrocked by flood,

the anti-intellectual purity in a Roman coliseum of lit crosses,
the benefits of centuries of belief in predestination and lower zero,

the counter-stirred poles of dissimilar parallel pitch and pulse,
the shock of blue blasts piped up and down streaming on spiral,

the days before medical birth riding a Ford axle turned by psyche,
bulked unknowing lifted into place by orange towering sky cranes,
community investment siphon-ups at knife-point privatized prow,
smoking first words of biblical sentences slipping from time-space,

the unusual rooms of sleep turning out dark in back of everyone,
the documentary film still showing on the other side of the sun,

the massive amounts of emergency water at the cold ocean floor,
troubled thresholds at underway horizons of old bison France,
masses that thicken and thin over moth-dust histories in matter,

old centuries of human longing in more than what was said,
the sparrow halfway seen we might have memorized as art.

FIRE SEASON IS OVER
TWO MONTHS LONGER

I.

Coastal storms will be further distorted by the naive
desire to be vulnerable to what must be heaven,
before it's been able to harden enough people to stone.

II.

Immense waves keep taking shells back to the first
laws of oceanic dumping: nothing much pays
with fire season crackling dry earlier into blowtorches.

III.

Planetary kindling has swooned up as driftwood,
dry as a hay fire raked through by the colossal
beauty of wood, flames, grasses, and distant suns.

IV.

More than one man has lived in a massive state
but failed to read any infinitesimal hubris
promoted at the bottom of the dissolving scene.

V.

The future world will be large and small in keeping
with the rational and intuitive, lit by substance
as by subtle thought, and with fundamental scarcities.

VI.

A lightning of future mathematics will bolt across
the sky from persons suddenly most vulnerable
the moment we must act instantly to save their lives.

DOLPHIN

I.

Rain and sunlight take shape in solid rock
with the feel of rocking that drains away
news, the relief of not having the nuclear flash.

II.

A dolphin soars twenty to thirty feet down
suddenly to rush up and leap into light
toward the ceiling of the renaissance cathedral.

III.

A roar echoes in distant sense, in the ambience
still around from when the universe began
this rumbling umbilical satellite-lit Friday sky.

IV.

A sea lion's bellow charges the chest
with late afternoon, fluorescent
and intricate, in crystalline impulse.

V.

There are unknown shut eyes in someone
trying to sleep by the sun-flared sea
waves in which trains burst out of the wind.

VI.

A western ceiling fan erases what may need
to be let go, iridescent, at the rugged
timberlines where you see why you'll stay.

STURGEON

An ancient sturgeon passes
by the viewing window
at the bottom of steps
of the dam on the heavy river
heading further into the west.
Suddenly the concrete mega-city
in the expected future has a scent
of magma. Potbelly 1940s air raid
searchlights are still tunneling up,
to scan the ceiling of oceanic sky
towering over the requiem.
The rugged private faces built up
over time into the aggregate rock
wall start to explain something,
but who has the ears to hear it?
Would these voices of rock sound
like the mother's when, carrying us,
she spoke with a friend, or primal
lizard etchings locked within a fossil?
Lifting beautiful curves of the human
shoulders and cheekbones still
being made for the mammoth body
of interlinked species keep breathing
in wind that rips and crashes
through the gorge behind us.
Has it come, the sturgeon, through
waterfall geomagnetic turbines
resounding at extremities of Earth,
to survive from long before
what's going on around here?

WHAT WAS FOUND

I.

He told us fish have hatched
with a single eye on a single head

the heavy metals talking
the earth frogs losing their grip

the marine conch shell spiraling out
more softly around a body, harder

to come by, the children's disorders
amounting, costing a family farm, two

families, three by the promising no one
keeps long, single cash on the single cash

shocked on foundations hauling that
which values start to stand for, barrowing

sanctity over hillocks as slipping
slippery rich conglomerations ignore

II.

Soon events are snagged from electrons
before they rest behind glass closed cases

the museum of open wealth unending
on other sides of what can be touched

the commonwealth a value in relics
but not in grass plants openly growing

the papers purchasing back, the dark
that brings its billowing belly shadow

high over cooling through and through
Pacific rain out in psychic ocean wakes

III.

When scent of burnt propane toasts
midnight in a wheel parts factory

oiled in some other country now, things
we need, the help for infirm, an army

gone away overseas, the troops lost
the hour stopped when the legs stopped

or part of someone darkened, sitting
in dark by the light and trusting

hope for whole brain, great wheat
the blood tests that might not have been

what might be still for thirty years
the many times now below knowing

IV.

Old cottonwoods power their roots
recovering even roads as gravity

of starlit snowfall leaves
through atomic core:

what might have fallen years before
quiet, propelled cool down

                              63

and then lifting, take Father
Abelard's Doctrine of Intentionality

when slowness reaches in, that
what we try to do

is most important, learning
later than we might what was

touched and what was intended
and how far ahead is it

MOSQUITO

I.

Mosquito, you maneuver your tactical helicopter by the ears of field cattle
    and people by the river where we're buoyant on vibrating strings.
Mosquito, do you know what you're drilling for as you punch into epidermis
    then leave behind a kind of bioslurry of invasive fracking compounds?
Of course, do people know what their own overpopulation is doing to others
    or to you as you morph in stages until emerging, a new form of being
    with adaptive biotechnology more efficient than what people can build?
Mosquito, we can barely see you unless we catch you and look through lenses,
    and people probably seem to you to be part of the bulk of nearby hills,
    while ingredients in our scent recall the green orchid you partner with.
I'm not a scout familiar with stagnant waters in which transformations occur,
    your wigglers turning into tumblers that burst into oil-drill helicopters
    out for blood to keep you making ova, rafts, and underwater snowfalls
    of tiny eggs in the possibility that a future exists, and yet who knows
    where our effects could be leading, given the brief lives we have here?
Mosquito, with your fifty varieties in the crosshairs just in this region alone,
    the Snow Pool mosquito breeds in meltwater, in stone basins of rain
    and condensation that has transpired from sister stoma of green leaves
    where being's vibratory, emergent, a negotiation that remains sound.
Mosquito, correct me if I'm wrong, but I reckon your life resembles people's,
    in the living of it, in deciding and being acted on, as day follows night
    that follows day, as every day inhales sunlight and the dark from before.
Mosquito, your bone-drill mating call's urgent, sad, as if your cells were saying
    your time's running out, which makes your lightning-flash sensorium
    quick and quickening almost in invisibility, as you attack what you love
    to ingest when not putting your face in a bloom or reaching into shape.
I hail you, mosquito, one being to another, not naming your kind or knowing
much about mine, but I say you aren't responsible for acts of relatives
such as those who killed half of our Vietnam War dead, and I had no

hand in draining the Black Swamp, as lethal as our hungers have been.
Of course, it's hard to see the harm we've caused, the way your kind spreads
    all the more fever the hotter it is – zika, dengue, West Nile, malaria –
    while people spill mixes of their 80,000 unnatural chemicals anywhere,
    and the latest studies show insects around the world are disappearing.
Mosquito, I know you drink nectar and blood so your species will survive,
    and yet my kind's gone further, ingesting entire bodies, even mammals.
I think I can see the world we've known reaching off the edge of the map,
    heat rising, disease vectors stretching, but as if a transformation
    were being reached for by large numbers of live species all at once.

                    II.
Missus Mosquito, come as quick as you will, missing as we've been.
We've reached the place where we stand, whatever we do, as standing
    flies in back of the seen and holding still comes over us
    from before, as stillness revolves around quickening of light.
Mosquito, you're drilling at high speeds into the living drum of my ear.
We've faced the mirror by diving through space to the future unknown,
    with our hungers grown in the open cracking into red-violet
    heights come down to where day thickens in spite of itself,
    burning out in flares along the rims of flying global water.
For this is the time before razor-blade dusk is severing ties to the day,
    when night exudes from the underground last to be first
    to block the passage of half-light burning out in graves
    exhaling smoke that's the absence of light leaving us still.
Mosquito, you fly before the red-violet dusk darkens down around us,
    drawing the last of day that pours through veins mined for gold
    where what we've known gives way, sleeping away in space.
Of course, it's being alive that knows what it sees, that uses these eyes.
And knowing holds onto the side of the world for which it was created,
    however crossed our purposes have been, as small as we are.
Mosquito, where we land, we swim. Where our cells have gone, we merge

with time that's easy to forget when caught in the middle of it,

when getting things done, people have tied fast knots in it,

as if parts of it would be doled out, as if big guns owned it.

But we participate, don't we, mosquito, from our cells out through light.

So our improvisation continues to thrive in the face of hard-wired forces,

in the sharp battle where your fighting spirit demonstrates

how to sit in the cockpit without forgetting the operation.

Mosquito, you're the product of flowing under-flowers hidden in swamps,

tiny blooms so green and quick they blend with the mosses

that power into the unknowable nutshell around gravity,

where you've been the protector of still waters and wild time.

THE FUTURE KEEPS MOVING THIS DIRECTION

Calls from the future continue in the empty place
where everyone meets. Oceanic fractals
can stir up a blizzard of uncovered shape, a procession
of walkers and trucks hauling photographs back into immensity,

the hand-painted Armenian masks and grandmother blankets
leaving old buildings wrecked by quantum lightning-first
ventilations of atomic space in the heavy historical cloud cover

at the receiving end where a serpent egg's cracked or black-box
elections have swamped pitch-dark crawls able to take you down
to where you began.

                        In the spectrum, sunlight delivers *will*
to animals trying what gives or how to take rock, as probability
falls into shape and cells with cardinal intent may be heading
off on impossible mass migrations from drought,

before anyone's reinvented complexity. Doesn't light drive down
from the beginning of beauty, shattering on contact with hair,
prisming with gas-ladling leaves plugged into nerve-center sky?

Doesn't each move of a leg, every laboratory chemical spray,
have its remote consequences most ancestors never considered
long back when nobody was aware of their microorganisms?

When flashes of impact start and end up splashing in torque
across pavement with ideational up-shifts in molecular
planetariums, methane gusts in cities of long-range disruption
of the climate already reveal uncountable
numbers in Dhaka North and Cordoba and more places

taking to the dust path, all they own on their backs
or in their arms, having undergone mountainous melts
and down-drafts of pulsatile swells flattening plants
in a spike of Celsius, with future footage showing a heat mirage

of great families crossing over from the thick of old-world ritual
into solar daylight as if it weren't anything, with shadows
of materialism as fall between temporal flux and a full meal.

IV.

Any person who loves another person,
Wherever in the world, is with us in this room
- **Kenneth Patchen**

Never forget that you are one of a kind. Never forget that if there weren't any need for you in all your uniqueness to be on this earth, you wouldn't be here in the first place. And never forget, no matter how overwhelming life's challenges and problems seem to be, that one person can make a difference in the world. In fact, it is always because of one person that all the changes that matter in the world come about.

So be that one person.
- **R. Buckminster Fuller**

SUITE: NOT KNOWING WHERE TO GO

✳

It's time to admit there's little I can do
about the recent scientific reports
of quickening Arctic methane releases

that could lead, perhaps in a few more years
but any year now, scientists are saying,
to an immense burp of the gas into the air,

enough of it to catastrophically strengthen
concentrations of heat-trapping carbon
quickly causing demise of flora and fauna,
particularly the animals with backbones,
which I believe includes people. It may be time
to say goodbye, so long, as long as I'm still thinking.

So goodbye to sweet unflowered Ophelia, and to Lear
with no castle left, chortling before sudden penury
under the black umbrella of his ancient thunderstorm,
and goodbye to the sea waves of inland golden wheat
reaching from the first root into wide streaming light
and global circulation of air.

                              It's certainly the only hour
it happens to be here, where being smack at the dark
bull's eye center of providence has placed all of us
naked before our effects – I know, however unintended
they were or ensnared everyone's been
by our weavings of unequal distribution.
Maybe we need more practice in the esemplastic arts of

demonstrating grace and blunt abstinence
when saying goodbye to one another and the culture too
early in the absence of suitable explanations,

and yet grieving forever the spectacular homo sapiens
tragedy would probably end up counterproductive.

✸

Incomplete complexity eats needle-sponged
trails along with cruising tour ships
of eastern mountain-top coal mine owners
for a snack, wolfing down toxic Gordian knots jammed thick
with ultrasonic Jesus navies working undiluted blasts
of thawed-down absentee tundra at the drop of a belt

until what violets make downtown reddening hang on
buildings as skeletons roaring with wind, feeding flames the last
light to reach the high plains where nighthawks are swooping
and diving in thermals for insects.

                                       Down the country road
to and from unthinkable works of international art
with solid yellows of Morris Graves corridors in extradimensional
nighthawk sweeps over the instantaneous drops off the brush
of aerial Pollock inscribing a tropical rainforest, where the charismatic
and tiniest co-evolved beings are holding up walls

of cells while being grows out in fractals that swoon upside down
if they need to churn more roil-outs until quickening
heaves up on Rorschach frequency maybe it is
from what comity in the dark knows pretty well.

For the present projects back and forth between mirrors in the split
second, as the matter in the mirror grows smaller with each return,
front mirror to back, to front then back, your head in the room,
the back of your head in the room, the front of your head in the room
of your head, in the room in the room, your head in the room
until you're small, so far away, far off in the back-and-forth mirror
with the rest you could never find it under the fingerprint night stars

undone shellacking the outmoded animal-horned illuminated texts
scanned by the Hubble, as the oceans crash one year into a next,
in material bake of the bioaccumulative prime exempting no one
from inflations of opposites or more unseen tundra thaws,
in the burn of bees maybe with the root roar elephantine,
ringing out of desire, a next century already moving broods
unlocked to mint soils of this chance operating in the back-roar.

                          For there's the sea-pumped wind
turning the sky on its capillary expanse with all its fertility
resounding, resisting the hard pack of clay, for uncountable
will be lives feathering back into the sea entangled with old thinking

pressured to fold into meditation on high Peruvian plateaus
amid exhaustion and the private Steller's jay in comprehension
wheeling through the onionskin atmosphere that arcs over
any prerequisites out of extravagance.

                          For touches of aphid's foot
will be taking dark-green swerves, heading away from Texas
that keeps guessing how hot it's likely to go
earlier every day of creeping sudden drought.

——

So this hungry complexity is out to scarf up what snakes out
benumbed onto solid rock in flame-high hills

for whatever stays to frame a candle of forethought
which spoons into the soup famished after weeks
of unusual psychic beauty

                              with natural hydraulics out in the sky
for miles in cost-benefit kitchens calving under live melts raw,
with re-enlistment engineered as evening lowers its dome of the sky
into an earthly rotunda before complexity swallows it all,

if only to remove the impediments standing between this rare life
and rural electric light in Western civilization revving up
unguentine wing-banners into fast-moving Egyptian fans
making displays at dusk of exotic Lepidoptera, when it's possible
a few had just blown in on sea winds with more than we knew
at that time, surviving on traces of matter and rain,
if it was a midsummer evening, in the breathing spectrum,
the arboreal dark with a full ancestral lift in deciding cells.

We've had quiet whispering of bulk loneliness,
as if rare Persian violas now were smoldering
in antiseptic tractor beams, snagged by razor wire
down here at the borders of ever-present infinity,
when it's just the lot of us when people sit down
before standing up and shaking off dusts.

✳

Here the electric cells in sprays of needles
are combing through the spectrum
for the root center of operations, mycelia,
arboreal rhizome, and soil sweetening in elastic time
with nightcrawlers under it all

knowing however the place looks with long-term mineral blends
that still reach into fin-making offshore at the tiniest levels,

                        for the good of the whole, are beings born
where the low cellular roar cracks up on the rock all day
into night in cradling air and the stay of germinating flux
bearing the mind that stands in a circle of people
the same as stone rising up in a circle of chiseled stone

for razor-edged time fans out at the coast, as primordial
insinuations launch into *gaining a little perspective* from eating
and trying not to be eaten, rotor flagellum whirring,
membrane-sails swollen, ballooned with undersea current
carrying salt-sea waters and the winds left going through crowns
of firs, propagating slow floods of incomplete calm, after panic
over not catching a breath with the compass needle pointing
        to the self that resembles inner dawn coming through
    the voices of animals which are music, and that cry on pitch

under the sun of Henri Bergson encompassed by improvisation
in the millions circling the planet around the likes of Klimt,
Matisse, or Gauguin sleeping with wild-haired beauty
in the unconscious which never stops being an animal

around high-end torque with low levels of basic
knowledge, given the damage done by the gods
the mammoth prophecy with primitive belief in ascension
and virgin birth and the human concept of solidness
as petroglyphs in what we call what we've seen
in the long-gone past that fills with emphasis.
For what happens next
takes on necessity.

✸

Torch-lit emptiness
leaves a wake
of photochemical reciprocity
between species of falling rain
and hurrying in light living
in the anomalous with heart-beat solar pulse,
hidden instrumentation of the likes of ants
raising aphids in the effortless simulations delivered by eyes,

the pre-existing exegesis of moth wing, wheat-wrenched
renewal of destiny over crazy, tendering transversals
down from heights to benefit barreling brethren purposes.

———

If the funeral of people goes silent in a back room
of the psyche, with a 100 million hammers
pounding in the coliseum of private ideas
that could be making little difference.

Haven't the crows and grackles always been stretching a wing over
anyone's paradigm collision?

                    On our shoulders, the atmosphere
soaked by oceanic humanity grows heavy. What happens next
could be tying your horse to a tree, where the new weather lands
consequences that demand at least one good eye within the mind.

———

More than one concert violin may have whispered fiercely
into your ear out of tenderness. The crows simply land
when it's the right time to let them go. For not a lot
can change the indelible present that's now your past,

when what's melting has unfrozen before our eyes forever.

However many symbolic mint condition fifty-ton earthmovers
are now parked on soft stretches of infrared profit,
it may not be possible to detect the shadow in the air
blanketed dirty by anyone's footprint
before it's gone off razing whole hillsides

where more intelligent cells will fly on wings
that advance by lifting themselves
and those watching over impermanence.

——

But the blue bowl will hold open
even for a private hour of loss
and continue through long pours of roundness,
worthiness, guilt or maybe remorse,
the blue bowl made to receive what the echoing
in it will hold at the hour of depth
in the orange-yellow earliness of dawn.

IN THE BREAK OF TIME

Anyone entering a room
has already stepped
through a threshold.
Anyone who lives between walls
has grown out of a tiniest origin.
Where you have being,
you have an extended moment
of being born. Everything happens
to exist in the only place it could be.
Now everything's changed.
Any person picturing a person
is alive on a planet in the cosmos.
The mind shows documentary
footage, as the brain entertains
presence. In the split second,
plants assist the planet undergoing
utter mitosis. Erasing long-term
indivisibility while embracing it,
the mind survives what the brain is
serving under the only tent in the sky.
Like the moon, longevity orbits
whales and the ants, gray squirrels
and the swift gold-brown foxes
of the foothills where being's born.
Whatever happens, whatever
has been working through presence
knows being blooms here and flies
as it swims. In the break
of time, a person's a prism
in the making of color
received from the root-pulse
spectrum within being quick.

PARTS OF THE FUTURE HAUNT THE PRESENT WHICH IS ALREADY PAST

Woodwinds and worms of matter reach into sunburst neural reception
out of swings of encompassing, in cycles at the root of reverberating
touch with phosphoric psychedelic capacities of quickened fertility

through long-skirted cellular acumen in heartbeat pounding lineages

with root-cloud working neocortex witnessing the medicinal bison flash,
this isn't the place our ancestors saw when framing what we learned,
where we've gone, when little would change the present now our past.

For the human head which remains a mushroom crowning in the yard
as carnival barkers croon to a Hammond organ, taking money at the exit,
the hoary yearning awash with gutted old-time belief lit by village torches,

the scorched ounces of regret smuggled past iron gates in genetic yards,

unjailing the guttural heliographics that pollinate revolving color wheels,
the urgent mass constructions out of classical traditions undoing profiles,
with scents of the topsoil we imprinted on when we were trying to walk

the sad vestiges of less-understood privatized childhood communion,
rudimentary choirs of giant Doug firs sounding out through space,
where mercy cultures appear in everlasting future tense of solar core,

the sea floors of sense under sleep in the mind, in the amber rise of sun

those who've opened or closed human eyes to the value of living species,
the unconditional beginnings of future mass migration, collective shock

straight in the scowling face of moray eel within everlasting future tense.
There's importance of everyone who lives, those who've grieved at a table,

the shock to aquifer industries of skinning then gutting outmoded belief,
the stay of what's leaving to live without notice in Antarctic readiness,
the rock of the sea behind its mask far back in spikes of chilled heat,

membranous swallows of indefinite passing afloat in a drop of hoo-haw,
the overturned back of straight-ahead meaning that moves sideways
when locked in gardenry of the eyeball iris in this body of momentum.

For this could be the day we foresaw from the pit of the hunger to love,
hearing the smallest thought ring with longing as aches our way ahead,
for we've had peak ciphered ligatures gone thoracic in sheddings of bells

unminded by neck-scruff leopard charges, cradled by cave-wall blanches,

the fathers' outmoded sense of freedom as something fishy gets richer
leading to public ethical necessity for surf-breaking points of no return
with spinning clock-room lifts of the molten core into a next foundation
for unpredictable skylines vanishing behind fresh penciled-in hatchings.

We've circumvented diverging approaches that lacked a common mind
around thriving hog farms of money, nursing shipping-crate streets
out of sacramental gaps in the fabric between feedlots and set tables,

for the ancestral mind in the city survives encyclopedic exactions of self

with an ear horn placed on a narwhal's chest to uncover guilt beginning
at elemental birth with the unmistakable agony you caused your mother,

when the human head cooked up by leaves understood it orbits the sun,
where we can't know the vision our parents had around our conception.

EVERY DAY WE LEARN MORE

Rodin stands strong in the body, as wisdom necessarily turns collective.

Every day on Earth we know far more about the centering nights
that come to terms with the corn-yellow present life, the human
                        global populations exponentially expanding,
bank accounts sinking, the hands in that dream that felt like swimming
                swearing to laws that may have been misguided, that permit
ownership of land,   when each person in a community is part of it.

The community has its factory time clocks wheeling on the teeth of gears.

This wouldn't be the first time breath has continued to be
what all species share, unless they're gone too high in the atmosphere
as test pilots without equipment can dive into heat
going up on the average thermometer
in spite of denying   the wildcat shrapnel that bursts out

            of multiplied directions as the brain remains loyal to the mind
melting where it has been melting as it's watering   to the bottom
of the slow-motion refrigerator edge   racing off
from ice face fronts quicker than the projections of computer models,

with large numbers of North American goldfinches of the new physics
at home in the open arms of cottonwoods   the scent of loaves
as 5 a.m. wafts into licking neo-Sumerian breezes off the great ocean.

For no one wants to hear the exquisite Cetacean name of the last whale
to spout on carbonic waters in sunlight risking the unknowable future

where craving in animals is well refined
as ritual moves, reenacted, sinking a central root   irreplaceable

as the air clears and hauls char on its way through swarming concentrations
as multiple pressures stand in the Sanskrit hum at the foot of plants,
in ashes of the evening river still pouring over medieval wolves and voles,
the mule deer consoled to this day
by St. Francis of Assisi at the calm center

with transience mollified by insouciance in all nakedness, in numbers
of thick-branched quark residuals giving shelter, places to live
in the morning air for the sake of patience   for what it's taken on

at the philosophic periphery of orbiting inextinguishable alertness
in the wild-haired conscious instant when the next present kicks in,

inherited sophisticated faculties unfurling at the genetic origin
adapting to volatility of conditions with scientific understanding
the moss-lit fortress of the rainforest where the air moves in being,

     in gusts going about their work of roiling up the long wing
       of rainfall raking over the seismic continent
         where archaic women before words
        would have given a long mothering thought,

burning out of electronic communication devices that abandon nature
as if animals in the wild were no longer singing the open song of air,
the miles kicking in sleep lanterns and Tibetan horns out of the mines
where digging beetles reside in the rod and staff first lessons of air.

For what you're seeing isn't necessarily there, here in front of you.
Not with digital blank-slate amnesia for the future in cosmic rays
quickening operations of the eyes capable of looking past thousands
of bulldozed parabolic receivers that have gone live with oyster pearl
vows in carp-throated spring-offs of the past, here on their own volition

thanks to emergency room doors that swung open
to offer resuscitation   in the only moment we may have
              where atoms are forever ticking down on their timeline
                  of unfinished sagacity, at times taking the road

past dairy ants protecting their sweet aphids under softness of mosses
      building in catalytically cracked independence to lightning-spun
solidness, when what can you do   if too much hasn't been done.

For you have your sounds of the expanse out of down-home Ernst
where the atmosphere continues breathing   over the millennia,
refining its translation, remodeling studios, adjusting to the moment
a straight-ahead spine surrounds with intrinsic newborn nakedness.

IN A SLEEP-DIVE SWOON

A few hell-hound whines out of Kerouac's astronomical
meat-wheel, and everyone's turned inside out, beyond
hot and cold, under revolutions of the more shamanic
stars in the dead of night, where rhythmic runic healing

can be hard to find in shadow canyons gone translucent
after 100-year downpours on the public plants of speech
twisted from close exotic torque of indigenous extractions
under a black umbrella, days before the end of the reign

of western identity from accelerations of unprecedented
simplicity holding large families hostage under cloaked
surgical-strike capability with its quick bird-swallowing
and brother-gutting, mantle-fracturing and big oil-drilling

business raking in untold hauls of spontaneous ice-cold
dogma moldering on Alpine mountaintops of microbial
sleep at work on what we've found when a sleep-dive swoon
spawns a fresh unseeable scripture of lying that cheats up

to reach future highs in an instant backslide at greater costs
to the present than what slips back in a generalized truck
borne of the harkened refineries in a tick-clock bison-flash
of Western supremacy denying sense exists for green-headed

mallards when unburdening the mother root of large money
around what might or might not survive archaic exposures
to temporal reddening which summons those who were born
for a long-term organic retrofit before half-buried inaccuracies

appear at the thunderhead edges in East European banks
of rain where the beginnings of Klee feather back into seas,
while global leaves comb power out of time, until it splits
into urgent public information uncountable eons from now.

LOCATION OF THE HUMAN HEAD

The human head clearly prefers its position
on top of the neck. It instinctively values
having the chance to see a little further
than if it were somewhere below. It can look
down, the head, and assess general condition
of the hands and feet, the chest and stomach,
the hips and knees, just in a glance. Perhaps
because the body is usually moving forward
or to the right or left, like a vehicle driven hard
down a highway, additional eyes never grew
through the back of the skull. But the brain
has invented a composite panoramic vision
that contiguously assembles based on its best
estimates. A quick slice of a longsword separating
the head from neck produces an exacting finality.
Rolling in dust, the mouth has nothing to add.
The eyes look at no one, not another warrior
or someone in the family. The head in this case
is a plucked apple, but without seeds to keep
the lineage alive. If detached from the evolving
cells that created it, the brain loses its mind.
Coordination of the fingers and thumbs ceases.
Blood gushes and pours from the terrible wound.
All purposes end with a squeezebox-whistling,
maybe it is. But the head secure on its original
neck observes what's happening and considers
its options. It seems to be home, resting its full
synaptic weight on the human neck and trunk,
 taking advantage of the view to extend time,
as it can, not only for itself but all that it loves.

THIS HOUR

Gills rake over the more remote undersea
pretexts stirred up out of the spiked
and contorted garnishments far down
in flux already operating in dark conditions

boiling over the lip of the petroglyphic spectrum
with a slime of oyster muds bearing current
hat swoops unshelled lobes past rostrum crags
bled purple under the not necessarily served
reciprocity in sea-slug subsensory delivery
to softened orange mouths of frilled sponges
mending copulative sea-slop saturated with salts

of emptiness in hard scudding sinks clogged cold
and indivisible as the light's weight breaking at limits
of penetration of the low from the tropical beyond
as a wave out of the forgotten, that arrived in widths
to carve into sunken stone the murky speeds of time

swerving past the full knowledge maybe we have,
but that instantly surpasses us, leaving a trail
of stripped steak carcasses, when we've found
more could be shareable than what others let on.

Therefore, out of being here within being, meaning
outlasts most suffered intensity, as old-growth
languages have sheltered us under heavy limbs
unfurling green solar labs.
                            Because breathing goes on
in action, but at the root remains more than willful,

we've had over a few million hammers pounding
in the financial colosseum, when not much
intricate enginery lasts around equal opposites
that continue to advance, as if this were the world

where you end up in the same place you began.

THROUGH THE CELLS

The state of the cells is they're alert, forever engaged
with flora in tinctures that arrived on trade routes
from which we've come not knowing which ancestors
may be influencing us now or what phantom old-world
whisperings may have come from a Byzantine ritual
incense stick bundler down the harbor from candles
of Pythagoras burning in the sanctuary of theorems.

Who were the forgotten first to be kind or to recognize
mindfulness in eyes? When forests guarded the fine-tune
fingertip touch, they promoted overflow communications
between disparate species with mint conditions operating
in the back-roar, in breath without trying, in the classical
days before medical birth.

                    Dusty keepers of irregular hours
must have had a keen sense of unexpected ways to fall in love
with vastness of night. Forebears who co-created what's seen
of the spectrum around cries for warm shelter of the mother,

cries invented out of urgency or shock over the emergence
of consciousness arriving from way back as well as ahead,
may have practiced their medicines when scouting
or hunting, and when sitting still in one another's presence.

Did the old ancestors walk as if they were entering a garden
that grows them out of much more than the mind takes in,
when hunting and gathering tribes of a few dozen must have
driven a hard past into palatial longings of mist, into Clovis
sharpening on blockages at the bar, with balked hamperings
or extravagant unity at conscious borders of the workday,

with preclusions and unrestrained hazarding, the cul-de-sac
impedimenta within arrested hitches or strict unhappenings,
before flagging moratoria or knaggier interdiction led on
to inducible renunciations arguing for chance surrender?

And yet we still receive word from the Mediterranean mother
of great great grandfathers who knew their long tree-trunk
boats on the waters, and mother of road-building warriors
who planted tons of stone markers with Roman numerals

when complying with rank pressures from the top meant
distributing them to virile weight-bearing micro-organisms
and heavier cornerstones known to the Swiss mechanic
or disciplined pianist good at math, the great grand aunts

who visited Parisian sidewalk cafes where intellectuals sat
sipping elixir, abreast with the news in heart-beat oneness,
in the encompassing of Henri Bergson expanding debates
of intuition.

          So Gauguin paintings could fill with emphasis,
dusk swept in where forebears followed footpaths long before
words and collected what they needed to give shape to hope,

since the human foot learned to swing out on its cantilever
and place itself down, the way it does now, nearly without
effort, without violating the first or last principles of residence

when prophecy wailed offshore in breakers where the soul is
contemplation resounding in spikes of gravitational *Existenz*,

when the young and laboring poor, the curious or banished
would have served as confidential witnesses of blood pledges,

in keeping with natural law, and managed to survive the heat
of extemporaneous rigors grave as the lyred angels in Majorca,

in gravitational gusts sibyl-smoked fast forward for generations
until finding us through the inherited fallacy of *all this is yours.*

V.

And so the new thinking now within the scientific community about the way genes and the environment interact is more like a piano with our genes as the keyboard, if you will, and the environment as the hands of the pianist. You could play Bach or you could play improvisational jazz – it's the same keyboard, it's the same DNA but the environmental messages have changed.

– Sandra Steingraber

I believe that we will see a lot of destruction, but I believe that if we can see the right patterns and draw the right lessons from that destruction, we might be able to rebuild before it's too late. And then I have that ultimate optimism that even if we can't, life will rebuild itself. In a way, the global economy might collapse, but Gaia won't, and people's ingenuity won't. We will rebuild society, we will rebuild local economies, we will rebuild human aspirations.

– Vandana Shiva

SAYINGS BETWEEN MELTING POLES

More than once you may have heard a practice whisper fiercely
    in tenderness.

Mothers of protection and bearings, our higher inclinations
    may have been infrared and swarthy at birth.

Work carries people on what hopes in a molecule.

Heavily invested identity may want to be seen swallowing a shot glass
    of what it's called two-thousand-year-old blood.

Present consequences require more than an eye alive in the brain.

Central nights and days let orchard paws survive the dark.

A barn of the ancestors sailed in, and was taken over by ants.

Countless ancestors had it wrong: fire was not an element.

Re-education of the mind is recommended for every decade.

Transmogrifications capable of supporting life occur in gardens.

Under philharmonic stars, unbroken strings of antiquity descend,
    touching almost nothing as they drop
      through unused space in atoms.

Is there a solution so the splits can again be whole?

This neural net with its speaking voice taps into more than it knows.

We have a few harmonic plasters in subsistence living at home.

A nervous branch loves as it dreads the wind's avocations.

A furious number of cajoled doubts possess wicked intelligence.

Beyond admitting intimidation or the relative size of a person
    in the cosmos, what can be tough for the mind
    is knowing the place is *home*.

We've given birth to an era thirsty and hungry enough to do for us.

The long-term still unfinished project of cells invented the brain.

More than once have buffalo-blooded bonds dampened the weave.

One note to the next on out to equity can be shocked by its catacombs.

Nobody's saying what not to do where or when to do what,
    as dawn breaks out in oceans of light.

The world shown to little children falls into and out of synch with time.

The fertile instrument lets the body ascend on trust of the genome.

Silent witnesses know a door flies open when the wild dream stops.

The nuthatch weighs almost nothing, while so much heaviness presses
    down around fern-combs of evening air.

It turns out history was written by half the brain.

Who has ever unearthed cheerfulness, particularly in a Pontiac?

Not all birds in back give others a chance, but many regulars do.

In the scent following a light rain, music rests on knowing.
97

Supercolliders pencil in variables for the energy apocrypha.

Yellow-orange lanterns in complex otherness ride
    in Ferris wheel gondolas that circle up
    then return to the ancestral underground.

A feather fills with sun, as gentleness ruins obscene palaces.

CROSSING

Out of the distance, the long-term train
that once was molten steel groans
when August drops its voice, passing stopped
ten-ton trucks and running up to the old
warehouses of uncrackable reinforced safes.
The lone diesel word for *steady ahead* or *always*
in between spreads across cornfields and builds
into a further 3 a.m. moaning call for the crossing.
Swallowing their tracks and the teeth of track-kill
the stacked engines roar through furious tunnels
of unknown future desert wind. The last-known
camouflaged Abrams tanks rumble underground.
Triply wrapped cases of embroidered blouses
go silent, passing anonymous as bleached coral
in a heart-sick bleat of warming ocean heaviness
in what the massive engines lower into night,
what reaches into the small neighboring houses
with rocking international rail cars that clatter
until they darken, where the long past is working
to rescind the latest, and yet not a lot appears ready
to return to any spiral whorl of higher intention.
The rushing sad morning and midnight
charge on. Blistering thin encircling gasses
reseed nuclear planets with time going off
each time erasing the fingerprint
night sky nebulae of human birth.

BUSLOAD AT THE METRO

A priest, a rabbi, and an optometrist walk into a bar. No, it's a station
    of the Metro, a massive marble-plated transaction lobby
    with vaulted cathedral ceilings in one of the decades
    when travel was still possible. So a priest in vestment, a rabbi
    carrying a briefcase, and an optometrist head in with others,
including a few fathers of mothers and mothers of fathers
    generating a charge that keeps the lights on,
along with an august figurehead stepping out of a frieze in a pavilion
    for the documentary on winning and losing all you can carry,
with an imaginary number of people who've been here before
    in a déjà vu in a déjà vu,
a sacrosanct primate-handler in a blond wig accenting
    her intricately tattooed tribal face,
a well-cut parapsychic invention in a cat-whisker vest sliding in
    the rotunda of a muted Gregorian umbrella,
a witness of chance situated on predilections for the grievously elated
    feed-lot stage,
an ancient misnomer in the making of dramatic forages in back
    of landholding,
a real Alaskan rolling her own in a writ of habeas corpus,
a slow snort of domestic whiskey promulgating song then bereavement,
a sunken side-pocket eight ball with an eye for the lacy fringe in purgatory,
a quick extraction emulsified in a concoction of wind-swept stilettos
    and black nylon country-western guitar strings,
a well-articulated speech overheard in medieval stone hallways
    of Macbeth's castle as Ginsberg's jukebox resounds,
a switch-hitter playing left field in a ball gown reinforced with tailor's pins,
    sporting an Easter hat nest in which Nepalese wrens are hatching,
a resemblance of 18th century corseting whose gown dissolved

in a future market fluctuation hand-in-hand with a master
    polo player skydiving into his now-impoverished home town
    where the secret's buried in a feed bag,
a lanced corporeal in a body of work and release,
a small tot dressed for an armored battalion that stretches back
    through time to the Roman Legion and Sparta,
a mild-tempered birthday suit cloaked by a team of industrial
    spoon makers Sufi-dancing,
with an in-depth artistic study of atriums from before the ancient
    Greeks to the present,
a reluctant domestic nude under an Etruscan hide serving a Lord supper
    plucked from the harp of Hellenism,
with a sizeable steer driving cowboys yonder as the sun sets into a little
    cowbird erupting with feathers where before there were none,
by a stunning underfed practitioner unbolting a tooth-whistled
    melodious extraction of common good,
with a penciled-in difference looking similar in light of the dooryard
    bloomed,
an uttering punch in the gut brandishing disarmament, smoking
    with pre-Caledonian ritual incense,
an off-hand bet on the risks of appearing with facial jewelry
    and ear bones humming out of their hymnals,
a shot at threading the needle eye in the company of top-drawer
    paparazzi in the kingdom of well-equipped camels,
with a child in a half-made somersault on spell-binding solar-lit
    Germanic soils,
a serious declaration in primeval galoshes angling straight back
    to the accounting department,
a nascent nay-sayer knocking around in a nanosecond,
an organic squeezebox released and recaptured by camp-tent idealism,
with a tough meander plowing up rock pouring toward the ocean
    where it's all headed,

an example of demand responding to the firearms community in a tall
    carcass of talking to a little question of upbringing,
a shipwreck survivor in a bottle,
a sauntering long engagement beside a state of betrothal negotiating
    an affair in small steps of garden-variety dalliance
    rubbing elbows with lovers of socioeconomic polyamory,
beside a polite kiss of the Pope's ring under towering rung bells
    from the book of large numbers,
a raccoon-hatted eager beaver still horsing around on the catwalk
    between one bull's eye and a next floundering only a little
    in the dog-gone room packed with wolf and lion-head
    pins on licking tongues of lapels,
a cozy previous approval in a leather vest and yak mukluks walking on eggs
    of threatened birds while the tundra melts,
a well of information tapping fossil aquifers left over from the Ice Age
    while dragonflies dart around her flashing eyes,
a few contemporary bald-faced tycoons of identity serving up a few more
    up-and-down hard congressional chews,
a generation gap that cracks further apart and consists of breaking
    current and high-rise transnational tankers,
a sip of East Indian tea in a milk-dull Victorian room standing off
    to one side in attendance with a sterling silver serving tray,
a rack of milk pushed to the lip of a backed-in truck,
a service employee on a transoceanic flight taken many times
    over to Berlin with its orange construction cranes
    lowering steel beams to beds of acetylene torches,
a pile-drive of the hard past like nobody's business with a strobe-lit case
    of dangerous religious tools,
beside a front door in a white vinyl car coat
    behind which archaic opposite energies rhawl,
with a major-league incapacity specializing in ignorance,
a hermetic overexposure to present effects, undergoing evolution

in gradual stages over scores of millennia,
and perplexity in the saddle of completion carrying out a violet
    for the fountain of delight,
a sounding board in a powdered wig, a croquet mallet in one hand
    and janitor's bucket in the other,
a ghost town rifling through secret pockets until his hands go numb
    and mule's braying with pity,
a hair-sprayed conquistador searching for purpose within longing
    for random distraction,
an honest believer laboring to maintain contact
    with otherworldly influences,
along with a little swing that flew out holding a young girl only
    to return twenty years later with three more.

DRUMBEAT THRESHOLDS

Withering and blossoming in the genome spreads. Where time delivers form unrecountable, the root of heat builds. Holds root in hatching mineral splits, as worm-holed undersoils pour within being in time out to the vanishing point rendered alive, hungry, and focused as the white eye of an aristocrat far back in the picture from old-world Flemish oils. Populations flood their cities in drumhead unison swells. Chemical-soaked topsoil dries in the till. Amendment ends in subSahara spreads, where the shorn and fleeced must rummage through hot wire and volts, where what once appeared to be unending ends.

———

In the fast grip of uncertainty maybe we were slow to notice charged engines of mitosis, the cumulonimbus lulls and scarlet-dark greased axles up-hammered by briny mathematics. Where ancient gyres have been wringing their hands, they've already been whip-snapping past classical vanishing points in the oils of history. Nothing we're looking at changes much, if not through renewable retooling, not without the cosmic axle overturning whole-hog incendiary integers standing in for identity. Rife with built-in pre-existence, maybe cold water sinks in externalized effects disseminate a tomahawk appeal nevertheless into tearlessness.

———

A spark-spitting bleached coral manifest spleen can end up dissatisfied in home-grown mammoth-with-opposites jolts, smoking and gnarled before shoulder-sleek future cries we've overheard halfway down in the hog-caked contagious dark. So the aftermath heads off into the gorge behind us, where wind's sharpening its blades and the highway circles an apple seed. When it's time to keep going at parabolic speeds, what's here remains indivisible from the whole. While graveyard punch presses with a blue-fin chance slam down with dumped arsenic ash reaching a valley-floor nerve, naïve beauty lifts a newborn, the naked equator racing around 100s of 1000s of the most vulnerable.

———

A thousand vehicles may not equal the exquisite complexity of a horse. The work of a wheel is never done. When seedlings reach a viable height, they begin to sing, and should from that time on be protected along with air. A hard rain falls in the future. Worry about Bangladeshis, and fewer North Americans listen. Mention the sub-Sahara, and the documentary fades. A medieval courtyard comes into view, where the queen is about to appear. Beauty in the genome protected by long-term learning follows her. Who hasn't been under her protection? Who hasn't imprinted on quick wing-beat hope? Who doesn't own the forests as a consequence of birth opening her eyes?

———

The same circulating global air that ritually masked antiquity defies the unobtainable. Long spins rounded out of affinity continue to imprint on the wilderness of Roman numerals steadily losing its animals. As calving melts swim into unbridled depths, collective intransigence remains unfinished and defenseless as swallowing in the small houses of sleep. Where what could become of us we could become, where kindness expands after the war, palatial belongings settle down lightning-first into harsh parallels of impermanence. Where desire's seen a top commodity, assumptions have left their out-worn apparatus, declaring it a resource necessary for growth. What appears to be growing with no end in sight has many thinking Earth is where life never ends.

Acidified-fjord under-the-foundation drill pressures top pretty-nice-day look-out-below saddening exacerbated by as-we-sit-here imbeciles crowing a swan song for attention, us grimacing idiots trained only for engine rooms of not saying much that makes you more enthused than transnational sexuality in implied continuing NASA, NOAA, EPA, IPCC, where you don't need to be a scientist to learn what may be shaping up, and therefore at stake for happiness to control this ice-melt carbonic for-I-have-sinned swimming-im-poverishment knocking upside-the-biomaterial-flues as the owls hoot in the remote ice-capped territory of unprecedented human endeavor. Drum-beat thresholds in the present abound. Suffering wants flare up. As sunlight comes through broken and whole.

The planetary core spins on the shading of a feather. Hungers unfold from archaic states of fluorescence in which centuries go down fast. The silence designating conscious borders brings more global impoverishment and medieval impregnation. Synaptic oper-ations touch as unconditional animals aware of what they're doing before words. From drivers' seats bearing ancestral intent have sur-round-sound tests of the climate been using an elbow out the win-dow. Blood-seeing traverses space between eyes of animals at the outskirts, when what rolls through the galaxy is desire, the desire for a little more – how do you say? – solidness in the face of fluid molecular bonds.

Unassisted eyes fall short, as facts on the ground assemble at unknown chemical speeds. The extra-temporal exists in living indi-visibility that humbles current definitions of self. The hour grows into a long time from one outbreak of hunger to the next. It turns out intentional ignorance almost feels like belief. A few dead bolts on fire doors may not have purposes other than shielding a child from burning shame or frozen hope. The vast experiment of the cells makes us a few billion hammers pounding in the massive coliseum of ideas. Old-growth trees voting in absentia raise security levels that fall through the spectrum of being, as what never happens rocks on its wild galactic wave.

———————

Each person who steps through the door makes the bell ring. Being revises the whole. Each person arrives in a burst. A few kids stomp off snow, or race ahead as the bell swings, going to town. The door shows up with a person drawn in by buttery light or scent of bread, the promise of pumpkin or words. A person is part of being, as being is presence expressed. The door opens as little kids pray, aurora borealis swirling at blood-brain barriers, old fathers carrying torches down the dark road. As sleep drops into dreaming the self awake, it's clear what animals mean to cells. The bell goes off, the mind's invested, and what works by dreaming has scripts playing. When all you want is to have a life, you borrow what's given, as people step through the door.

———————

A greater invention than large or small has already whispered fiercely. Long-standing ache grows amber-gold wheat, as moths have opened their wings into manuals of dust far from want. Single-winged halibut swim through imperative, where the usual road goes off, leaving everyone in Rouault outline. With means of production returned to local hands, climate disruption leaves fewer harmed. Aching in the spectrum spreads through unforeseen thermals and cottonwoods smoldering with rain. *Nothing to see here* is tacked up around peace vigils at the front, with pallets of culturally activated incendiary devices aching the mind alive.

———

All day the sky's seen and yet not. The void lobs lightning into the gene pool, soaked with prairie protocol. Urgency swerves into the turn until it's a few feet from the door, its Hummer revved in neutral, the faceless driver about to shift into drive. Is this a neighborhood where the mind wants to see what it knows? A man in a bomber jacket sinks his silhouette into the café window of the "Hymn to Joy," part of him back in the sub-Sahara burning oil or talking on phones about effects of the drought. Isn't that tree a blizzard of moss? Is the forest stored within seed? Wouldn't this be the spring meadow unremembered fast in a drop of rain?

———

What may be within us, simple as we are, what could go wrong, contending with basic hot and cold, practicing for yellow-gold dawn in longing, in long-falling rain, where the species is, living larger than necessary out of this anomalous and effortless heart-beat in an instant, around oyster-lit Neolithic snail spindles of laboring repast within the wild sweet Sitka unfinished hour through state-of-the-art current silence, at resounding conscious borders of bone down rock of the horizon and rare birth you were ready to inhabit in your time, in a burst of what cells know is a wide-open, very quick time.

ORCHARDS AND BONES

Fresh bread that finds hunger, old sky and root,

praise enough, where the job's taking you,

externalized red center gravitas,

forgetting that carries in its process,

shoestring grief over pungent sprays of cedar,

irreducible cottonwoods that climbed

out of underground history,

shape reweaving out of tiniest animals,

tortoises of force in decision,

recovery breaking back into costs,

smoldering golden boots worn in the courtyard of pollen,

long hair in the dusk, where it towers,

streetlights revealing lobed and shaded presence,

swerves of gunned sedan,

shoes picked over on the public rack,

the continent that reddens and saddens,

exactness out of range of the Italian renaissance,

the be-numbered manifest wants,

rock in the trunks, where petals fall into accumulation,

skylines of Aztec neuroleptic predilection,

the rutted and heavy bindings and bone,

relative inarguable burns and Miro,

the handbell filling its belly with lit candles,

presence pulsing in absence,

the branches of speech rooted in mercy,

earnest mirrors filled with sun,

planted beams in efficiency,

night in the hills where roots show their orchards,

risk, with the white door open at the top

of the staircase in Gothic spires,

miles of arrival in anything seen,

the waterlogged 1800s in swamps the oceans flood,

the far-off eyes in company corn,

softening long-headed ox gazes we carry,

feathers of low-ceilinged sun,

years before all has been said.

THE IDEA OF MORE GASOLINE

Since the ground must bear upper strains of zero
in parts of itself, the next century's past grows
dark-brown eyes. Collectives of yellow-and-black
evening grosbeaks fly between mammoth climbs
of the elk. In the historical context of condor eggs,
duplicity haunts a few southern power companies
capable of burning great numbers of fallen angels
for firewood as they block the new grid, simmering
in long soups of animal resistance at the pleasure
of exceptionalism. Further generations of human
weight surely will follow, hauling in an additional
panthery insistence of hunger and need, multiply
adding broods of civil inception and advancing age,
to the arterial traffic within carbon-winged libraries
of congress. Heat grows with spikes and disruptions
around us, in pipe-backed sloughs and landholding
takeovers, alluvial drifts and coastal work – where
many women and men will be seeking places to live.

THE IDEA OF ALLEN GINSBERG

It's quite difficult to picture Allen Ginsberg as one
of the neighbor boys or someone who's dead now
but remains alive in numerous minds of my generation
and minds my generation has taught or influenced
in a café, where authentic expressions in syntax
may breathe in speaking until they seem to have life,
and the author's being discussed in present tense.

It's harder still to imagine Allen Ginsberg studying
humanity over time, across cultures, playing harmonium
to the gravelly *profundo* out of his fathered-up singing
of yellow-paged Blake, journeying in vehicles of Detroit
coast to coast on the turn of a month or two of jukeboxes,
investigating the overcoat and derringer agency of Central
Intelligence with human rights under its surveillance,

or flying on a Trans-American jetliner with Ferlinghetti
to a Prague stadium to deliver urgent lost disappointment
and latest arousals before tens of thousands hoping
to find the Beats, after reaching Western depths in *Howl*
and *Kaddish* that heightened speech in designated recesses
of bald-cheeked commissaries, before and after plumbing
heights cross-legged with Chogyam Trungpa in Tibetan
conjury and Black Hat recreation of Buddha's breakthrough,
with mandala offerings of the ritual continents returned
by monks to the river. But seeing Allen Ginsberg with eyes

awash by the river of bucks that followed Reagan's selection
of funds in middle-class hands to be siphoned up big time
by expanding wealth might not pan out. In explorations

of consciousness, after years working as "a psychonaut,"
while he contemplated what was around him in modern
and ancient contexts, did he reach a point he had to admit

errors of his ways? Did he shave his chest, comb his hair
back like Michael Douglas in *Wall Street*, then apply himself
at Goldman Sachs? Did he soar to heights of investment
and thrive in electromagnetic echelons of PR firms, devoting
his imagination to lucrative campaigns, donating his brain
to material distributions on the side of supply? Did he see
the futility and absurdity of dedication to writing and,
calling us *consumers*, declare the victory of materialism?

PUSH

The onrush of surviving like no tomorrow,
the start-up of imperative like no return,
the downward dreaming Motorola *prima materia*,

the cross-generational meteor crater of nastiness,
the grinding-down gears surrounding the nativity,
the beautifully whole openness and half ignorance,

the deepening neural swim of autonomic intelligence,
the driftwood mammalian sculptures seawater has
shaped over many years that already have been lost,

the parliament of healing spectrum of fierce collaboration,
constructions of organizational moss compound wait
at the origin of grief for the future we'd be leaving undone,

moving at speeds of scarlet-cured turns of in-house gravity,
the ocean's stone-ground give of short stacks of temporal
smoldering contracted impure, widely unformed invisibility,

the massive closed and opening first-felt saturations burning
and watering, the roosted chain-linked abeyance ongoing
and gone into the hot and diamond-cold embrace of an ocean
talon, the blunt revolution of wheeling blades taking stabs

at central authority, the streaking alarm that fails to dissolve
in enough time or no-time, the efficiency at which advances
overtake witnesses and wastes of boilerplate responsibility

in the trash burns behind rendering, the disusual stroom
of Sabbath forbiddery, the vulnerable hungry sea-weight
lost or serving the incomplete commutations of inception,
surviving commons, or forsaken thrills of the continuum.

GIVEN A LIFE

Flagellum materialize where tiniest beings have been
reaching out of eons, conducting business, moving
to stay alive. Smallest breathing mobilizes over time,
swoons blowering *en mass*. Evolving microorganisms
prism in the spectrum, while the documentary reveals
infinitesimal choices in slow motion. Once people have
congregated, involuntary hunger runs oil-hot carnivals
as normality pays admission. River current continues

in circulation of blood building complexity in the brain
to field the complexity around us. Through distances
and intimacies, the brain practices its arts that began
long before birth. Forebears inside us carry a fondness
for harpsichord and seasonal heat. In burning basement
libraries, Freudian entanglements reinvent communion
through the emergence of fundamental consciousness.

Many have imprinted on what used to be, each moment
of cosmic origin launching into what it'll never again be.
The pin-drop dark blurs what it touches, then absorbs it
in eclectic soup-pot horoscopes, the way it is, wanting to
live, to continue in being, to be here where listening
resonates through transcendence letting the world go.

SENTENCES TIED TO A TREE

Marines charge up on shore in the spectacle of humiliating angry fathers.
Blank-slate fertility sky-rockets following the concert of sky-burned coal.

Along the edge of mercy, the ocean of beings is out erasing comparisons,
as the blistering cave-wall instant draws the eye to the vanishing point.

Stallion rivers that pour through the sky appear ready to fall on anyone.
Roman numeral countdowns continue to march upon medieval villages.

The King's English may have consoled kindly guards at the ancestral gates,
but what's so good about waking if it doesn't build its roads to dreamtime?

Sweeps of intent roll in waves only so far before causing national borders.
Halibut swim on their single wing past jokers and exotic foreign queens.

Where the toddler's familial spoon will be filled one second, empty the next,
disproven Western assumptions that cannot be retrofit must be scrapped.

Will materialists never tire of dressing up in ever more African diamonds?
Dick the Bruiser sure could transfix the Sheik with a sweaty hammerlock.

Soundtracks that scar childhood recall end up a few remnants of identity.
If it weren't for the human head, wouldn't everyone have more of a clue?

Suddenly the small toddler's lunch spoon is being used to beat the drum.
Transcendence flies over on vanishing wings where the Earth turns green.

SINGING OF THE MICROBES

Embracing the microscopic creatures in our midst can be tough
enough since not all the people in the city walk around viewing
the place through a high-powered microscope, and who can hear

what microorganisms discuss or pick up the lyrics if they belt one
out of cellular mitosis while small seeds search for soft landings.

The wheeling center unloosens rings within rings, then goes on
cross-sphered, hugging turns, turning into fundamental mystery.

The way occupying alien forces at some points have been seated
in the unfinished hour, hammering into beatific marrow, steadfast
on hill-shoulders the red waves keep embedded when crawling up

to the riddle of the Sphinx long before its naked and insurmountable
exotic face stood scoured by army winds and dry-blown suffering
under bondage gone off shot out in flare-ups of such a cold cat-eyed

universe so cardinal in concatenation it was born vacuum-shattering.

So the Sphinx stands instantaneous, as deity, as if a galactic landing
had happened but so long back it's buried under soil-tendered sleep
lanterns out of pulls and spring-offs in root hum under long-forested
stretches of sharp wing promoted over its gut opposite, streaming

out of the ears of species night-listening below the flash of unfurling
mineral bursts on the slightest rolling slopes of lineage bawling silent.

So we were able to arrive at the scene of Crusades that aimed to employ
the horsemen of medieval war to liberate the Middle East from forces
that disturbed stability of certain arms-slinging knights who required

the origin of their white superiority to stand under Western control,

biblically speaking, and we've taken in the bazooka-beriddled Sphinx
in recognition that it's under the long-aging spell of its blank-slate
amnesia for the future, for hundreds of grueling long-colonized years

for which reparations are owed, years that now must finally surrender
across rising oceans of language, leaving all weapons with the Sphinx,
then revealing all vassal-polished tools in upside down photographs
of stolen riches justified by making exploitation a backwards salute

for risking their lives embattled before the glass emergency room doors

locked on subsensory pulse with tenacity that sells itself off for a price
that's high but been thought balanced on anyone's taste for small talk.

So the lion lungs out of cosmic bursts expand in honey-pot forbearance,

leaving a felt trail of grave genetic encryption from cracked-apart wants
that do the bidding for heavy wealth, as bald-faced as impermanence
that forgives the lot in a cherry-scarlet forever fomenting out and back

not in one place only, but reeling in spikes wrapped around each ounce

of tenderness, call it, in front of long mirrors in the exquisite machinery
of old science assembled where philharmonic violinists drew on depths

of collective Stonehenge reception, stirring up more possible ancients
driven mad into inventiveness by the largesse of mushroom imperative,

ticking the time in their heft down to zero, and not out into the expanse.

Thus, we were able to discover heart-beating ebullience in an unfinished
drop of bright silken water tracking the edges of nuclear slopes as rivered

and swimming as when we recovered the vision of neurological Ernst
from the days he went bell-sloshed in the shuck of gone disequilibrium.

AFTERWORD

Many resources are becoming scarce but none more scarce than time.
– Lester Brown

1949. When some of us were born, approximately 2.5 billion people were living on the Earth.

2020. Around 2020, while the worldwide headcount eclipsed 7.8 billion, a question anticipating planetary conditions in 2045 was posed on Quora: "What will be the main problems when the world population reaches 9 billion?" A reasonable answer, consistent with facts, trends, and expert analyses, was given by Preman Tilson of New Zealand: "Climate change. Overfishing/ocean degradation. Resource scarcity (water, food, etc). Refugees and political unrest. Pollution and urban crowding in those countries that continue to experience booming population (mostly Africa, Middle East and South Asia)."

"Climate change," of course, is a quick way to point to the polar ice melt, absorption of more solar heat by dark water (formerly reflective ice), warp of global circulation systems (the Atlantic ocean conveyor at risk of shutting down, causing a permanent European freeze and other effects), exponentially warming oceans, sea-level rise threatening major coastal cities, more energized storms, floods and drought, heat spikes or "domes" (such as 2010 plant-killing temperatures in the Moscow region), failing states (unable to grow enough food or to buy it on the global market, with armed gangs filling the void and climate refugees forced to seek new homes), the spread of disease vectors, release of microbes and methane from thawing tundra, fizzing blocks of frozen methane (clathrates) melting for the first time since people have walked on two legs (clathrates Arctic experts think could thaw en masse, shifting the processes into overdrive), loss of species, and much more, including elevated heat itself causing hardship and deaths.

Many plans to mitigate the climate problem and strengthen community resilience (the ability to withstand unavoidable shortages or environmental difficulties) can easily be found, particularly in the expert-written multiply reviewed reports of the UN's Intergovernmental Panel on Climate Change (the IPCC) and in books such as Al Gore's *Our Choice: A Plan to Solve the Climate Crisis* (2009), Paul Hawken's *Drawdown* (see the interview on *Yale Environment 360*, "Paul Hawken on One Hundred Solutions to the Climate Crisis"), and Lester Brown's *Plan B* or his subsequent books. Mitigation and adaptation are also discussed in detail on many sites – of note would be "Stanford engineers develop state-by-state plan to convert U.S. to 100% clean, renewable energy by 2050" by Bjorn Carey and Mark Jacobsen's The Solution Project, NASA Office of the Chief Scientist and NASA Global Climate Change (see Solutions), the usgdb.org Guide to LEED certification (Leadership in Energy and Environmental Design), www.bcorporation.net (the triple bottom line), the Natural Step (strategic sustainability), and many others.

From what I can determine, the changes that must be made are happening, but not at the rates or levels we need. Lester Brown has always called for mobilization at "wartime" speeds. But it's almost as if a cultural force were blocking immediate action, even stopping people from recognizing the climate emergency. And indeed it has. Geoffrey Supran, research fellow in the History of Science at Harvard, together with Naomi Oreskes, Professor of the History of Science, published a series of studies on the climate communications within ExxonMobil. Supran summarized the findings for the *Harvard Gazette*: "The takeaway message across all of our work is that over and over, ExxonMobil has misled the public about climate change by telling the public one thing and then saying and doing the opposite behind closed doors. Our latest work shows that while their tactics have evolved from outright, blatant climate denial to more subtle forms of lobbying and propaganda, their end goal remains the same. And that's to stop action on climate change." "Superabundance" is part of this effort.

Or see the Union of Concerned Scientists' December 7, 2021, article ironically titled "Oil Execs Spout Disinformation at House Climate Disinformation Hearing." What is it oil executives don't understand about climate-induced suffering of the most vulnerable people on Earth and the risks to life itself? To be sure, many lawsuits are in the works, but how much time do we have?

2023 and Counting. The Worldometer list of World Population by Year reports the present total number of human beings is 8,045,311,447, while the Census Bureau's World Population Clock at the time of this writing hasn't quite reached 8 billion. What we know is that the counts will continue to increase as will the load of carbon compounds we're releasing into the air. Temperatures are rising, breaking records, and many people today still subscribe to values and assumptions that have taken a toll on ecosystems, the climate, and the chance people will get along. Shreds of plastic in the acidified oceans will soon outweigh sea life. Biologists warn that the Sixth Mass Extinction is already underway. As we know in Oregon, we're seeing a new generation of climate-exacerbated wildfires. And, of course, we've painfully noted signs in this country of the sorts of political turmoil that could run around with its head cut off if unprepared communities experience scarcities.

In the face of so much damage to systems that support life, what can we do? The place to start is the IPCC Summary for Policymakers, coupled with a sound rejection of ultraconservative politicians who've had many people swallowing their own futures in roils of arrogant juvenile potshots taken at people who call for change or who value the common good. We must pursue what we know is true and work to advance civilization through sciences and the arts and the use of reason, while referencing facts on the ground. Archconservatives without platforms have failed to understand their roles. Since Reagan, they've pursued their own economic gain at the expense of all else but claimed to stand for voters. In recent debates they've laughed like imbeciles at the idea of climate change.

In a time with so much derangement on the loose moving from air-conditioned room to air-conditioned room, it's incumbent on people of good will not to lose sight of the facts.

Will the poetry of this era be like its politics, subordinate to feelings, or will it reach for a unifying ecological vision? Can poetry even live where the future's disappearing? The picture plane is no longer nailed down, and most of the picture may be out of the frame. The greenhouse gasses, the plastics we pitch, and points of view that assume superiority of the human over complexity of the creation have consequences that continue around the world. We can see what we're doing, but not necessarily what we've done. To be sure, exploitation of beings and ecosystems is a moral failure that promotes economic inequity, fails to recognize the intrinsic value of other people and species, spreads arrogant beliefs that people do not need the world (that they can live anywhere, even on Mars), and swears people thrive in competition, not collaboration.

But poetry asks who really owns the land under the lawns. Poetry understands that the world is inherently interconnected, that what appears before our eyes continues around the bend. My hope is that the poems in this book come across as music, that the extended passages are integrative and insistent on exploring perspectives. This book is dedicated to you and to the other species with whom we share the planet, beings who are as much parts of us as we are part of them.

James Grabill
Fall 2023

ACKNOWLEDGEMENTS

The author gratefully acknowledges publications in which these poems and prose poems originally appeared (at times in other forms):

Arabesques (Algeria): "Fractions Lit by Sun"

Axoloti: "Location of the Human Head"

The Bitter Oleander: "Shadow of the Fires" (as "Bonfire Shadow")

Calapooya Collage: "Sturgeon"

Caliban Online: "Busload at the Metro," "Going On before Going," "Push," "Smoldering Wing-Beat Swells," & "This Hour"

The Cape Rock: "Hunger Turns Heavy"

Deluge: "Uncertainty"

Elohi Gadugi: "Drumbeat Thresholds"

Gargoyle: "In a Sleep-Dive Swoon"

Glassworks: "Crossing"

The Grove Review: "What Was Found"

Gulf Coast: "Cut of the Blade"

Hamilton Stone Review: "Given a Life"

The Kerf: "The Divine"

Many Mountains Moving: "Fire Season"

Manzanita: "Western Matter and Energy"

Mountaineers Books, *Cascadia Anthology*: "Mosquito"

Otoliths: "Every Day We Learn More"

Phantom Drift: "Bottleneck" & "Sidewalk Violin"

Raven Chronicles: "In the Break of Time"

Red Earth Review: "The Idea of More Gasoline"

Skidrow Penthouse: "Puritan Matters," "Steaming Fields," "The Future Keeps Moving This Direction," & "Wave of Light"

South Dakota Review: "Orchards and Bones"

Stand (UK): "Dolphin," "Freefall," & "The Idea of Allen Ginsberg"

Survision (Ireland): "Sentences Tied to a Tree"

Unlikely Stories: "Muscled off the Plane," "Onward Business Soldiers," "The Job of Pharaoh," "The Time of a Few Gargantuan Nest Eggs," & "Through the Cells"

Waxing and Waning: "Remains of Being Awake"

Willow Springs: "The Queen Joins the Banquet"

The author wishes to express appreciation and gratitude for L. Bernstein, W. Marsalis, R. Shankar, & A.A. Khan; to V. Van Gogh, W. Kandinsky, M. Rothko, & M. Chagall; to B. Dylan, N. Young, J. Mitchell, & Lennon & McCartney; to G. Kinnell, G. Snyder, R. Bly, & P. Neruda; W. Whitman. R.W. Emerson, & T.S. Eliot; to B. Tremblay, C. Howell, D. Sheffield, H. McCord, L. Smith, B. Mohr, J. Tipton, J. Otto, D. Memmott, M. Schumacher, & B. Witherup; to P. Petersen, D. Averill, V. Orr, & B. Siverly; to J. Bradley, G. Kalamaras, P. Woods, R. Gonzalez, L. & J. Zimmerman, & Leon; to B. LaMorticella, J. Kaady, J. Sherard, W. Carlile, & M. Nelson; particularly to D. Raphael for ongoing friendship, wisdom, and ideas that helped shape this collection. And most of all to Marilyn Burki – for ongoing encouragement, engagement, our home, and love of the arts & other species.

ABOUT ATMOSPHERE PRESS

Founded in 2015, Atmosphere Press was built on the principles of Honesty, Transparency, Professionalism, Kindness, and Making Your Book Awesome. As an ethical and author-friendly hybrid press, we stay true to that founding mission today.

If you're a reader, enter our giveaway for a free book here:

SCAN TO ENTER
BOOK GIVEAWAY

If you're a writer, submit your manuscript for consideration here:

SCAN TO SUBMIT
MANUSCRIPT

And always feel free to visit Atmosphere Press and our authors online at atmospherepress.com. See you there soon!

ABOUT THE AUTHOR

JAMES GRABILL's writing appears online at *Calibanonline, Unlikely Stories, Terrainonline, The Decadent Review, The Vital Sparks, Otoliths,* and others. Since the early 1970s, his work has appeared in periodicals such as the *East West Journal* (US), *Toronto Quarterly* (CAN), *Harvard Review* (US), *Greenfield Review (US), Willow Springs* (US), *Seneca Review* (US), *Caliban* (US), *kayak* (US), *Phantom Drift* (US), *Stand* (UK), *Poetry Northwest* (US), *Oxonian Review* (UK), *Magma* (UK), *Plumwood Mountain* (AUS), *Common Review* (US), *Momentum* (US), *Urthona* (UK), *The Buddhist Poetry Review* (US), *Shenandoah* (US), *Chariton Review* (US), *Laurel Review* (US), *North American Review* (US), *Verse Daily* (US), and *Weber: The Contemporary West* (US), as well as many others. He received a B.F.A. in creative writing in 1974 from Bowling Green State University the first year it was offered and an M.F.A. in creative writing from Colorado State University in 1988, again the first year it was possible there. For a number of years, he taught writing and literature including the Shakespeare sequence for two years. He team-taught in the Clackamas Accelerated Degree Program (for folks at least seven years out from high school and employed full-time, often with children) and helped develop a year-long sequence in which he taught systems thinking and global issues relative to sustainability.

www.ingramcontent.com/pod-product-compliance
Lightning Source LLC
Chambersburg PA
CBHW021547150726
47990CB00006B/2427